The Node Craftsman B

An Advanced Node.js Tutorial

Manuel Kiessling

BIRMINGHAM - MUMBAI

The Node Craftsman Book

First published: April 2017

Production reference: 1260417

Published by Packt Publishing Ltd.
Livery Place
35 Livery Street
Birmingham
B3 2PB, UK.
ISBN 978-1-78712-814-9

www.packtpub.com

Credits

Author

Manuel Kiessling

Acquisition Editor

Dominic Shakeshaft

Technical Editors

Devesh Chugh

Nidhisha Shetty

Indexer

Aishwarya Gangawane

Production Coordinator

Arvindkumar Gupta

About the Author

Manuel Kiessling is a software developer and IT manager living in Cologne, Germany. He's interested in Behaviour- and Test-Driven Development and Agile practices. Manuel has authored many successful books including *The Node Beginner Book,* and *Beginning Mobile App Development with React Native.*

www.PacktPub.com

For support files and downloads related to your book, please visit www.PacktPub.com.

Did you know that Packt offers eBook versions of every book published, with PDF and ePub files available? You can upgrade to the eBook version at www.PacktPub.com and as a print book customer, you are entitled to a discount on the eBook copy. Get in touch with us at service@packtpub.com for more details.

At www.PacktPub.com, you can also read a collection of free technical articles, sign up for a range of free newsletters and receive exclusive discounts and offers on Packt books and eBooks.

https://www.packtpub.com/mapt

Get the most in-demand software skills with Mapt. Mapt gives you full access to all Packt books and video courses, as well as industry-leading tools to help you plan your personal development and advance your career.

Why subscribe?

- Fully searchable across every book published by Packt
- Copy and paste, print, and bookmark content
- On demand and accessible via a web browser

Customer Feedback

Thanks for purchasing this Packt book. At Packt, quality is at the heart of our editorial process. To help us improve, please leave us an honest review on this book's Amazon page at `https://www.amazon.com/dp/1787128148`.

If you'd like to join our team of regular reviewers, you can e-mail us at `customerreviews@packtpub.com`. We award our regular reviewers with free eBooks and videos in exchange for their valuable feedback. Help us be relentless in improving our products!

Table of Contents

Preface

About

The aim of this book is to help beginning JavaScript programmers who already know how to write basic Node.js applications in mastering JavaScript and Node.js thoroughly.

Status

This book is finished and will only receive updates regarding errors. It was last updated on January 26, 2017.

All code examples have been tested to work with Node.js 7.4.0.

Notes on code formatting

Please note that long lines in code examples may receive a line-break, denoted by the backslash sign \. Take care to put those lines into your editor as one line.

Take, for example, this code block:

```
dbSession.fetchAll('SELECT id, value, categoryID FROM keyword \
ORDER BY id', function(err, rows) {
```

The PDF version of this book shows a line break right after the keyword part, denoted by a \ after the keyword.

However, in your editor, you need to make sure that the whole code resides on one line.

Also, note that from what I can see, code blocks can not be copy-pasted from the PDF version of this book. While this might seem like a major annoyance, experience shows that learning to program works way better if one is forced to transcribe code from a book into the editor.

Intended audience

This book will fit best for readers that are familiar with the basic concepts of JavaScript and have already written some basic Node.js applications.

As this book is a sequel to *The Node Beginner Book*, I recommend reading it before starting with this book.

Part 1: Node.js Basics in Detail

Introduction to Part 1

The goal of this book is to enable you to write Node.js programs of any level of complexity, from simple utilities to complex applications that use several external modules and consist of several layers of code, talking to external systems and serving thousands of users.

In order to do so, you need to learn about all the different aspects of Node.js – the tools, the methodologies, the libraries, the APIs, the best practices – and you need to learn how to put all of that together to create a working whole.

Therefore, I have split this book into two parts: A collection of different basics in this part, and a thorough tutorial on how to put these basics together to build a complex application in `Part 2`, *Building a Complete Web Application with Node.js and Angular*.

In Part 1, every chapter stands on its own and isn't directly related to the other chapters. Part 2 is more like a continuous story that starts from scratch and gives you a finished and working application at the end.

Thus, let's start with Part 1 and look at all the different facets of Node.js software development.

1
Working with NPM and Packages

We already used NPM, the *Node Package Manager*, in order to install a single package and its dependencies for the example project in *The Node Beginner Book*.

However, there is much more to NPM, and a more thorough introduction is in order.

The most useful thing that NPM does isn't installing packages. This could be done manually with slightly more hassle. What's really useful about NPM is that it handles package dependencies. A lot of packages that we need for our own project need other packages themselves. Have a look at `https://npmjs.org/package/request`, for example. It's the overview page for the NPM package *request*. According to its description, it provides a *simplified HTTP request client*. But in order to do so, *request* not only uses its own code. It also needs other packages for doing its job. These are listed under `Dependencies: qs`, `json-stringify-safe`, and others.

Whenever we use the NPM command line tool, `npm`, in order to install a package, NPM not only pulls the package itself, but also its dependencies, and installs those as well.

Using `npm install request` is simply a manual way to implicitly say *my project depends on request, please install it for me*. However, there is an explicit way of defining dependencies for our own projects, which also allows to have all dependencies resolved and installed automatically.

In order to use this mechanism, we need to create a control file within our project that defines our dependencies. This control file is then used by NPM to resolve and install those dependencies.

This control file must be located at the top level folder of our project, and must be named `package.json`.

This is what a `package.json` file looks like for a project that depends on `request`:

```
{
    "dependencies": {
      "request": ""
    }
}
```

Having this file as part of our code base makes NPM aware of the dependencies of our project without the need to explicitly tell NPM what to install by hand.

We can now use NPM to automatically pull in all dependencies of our project, simply by executing `npm install` within the top level folder of our code base.

In this example, this doesn't look like much of a convenience win compared to manually installing `request`, but once we have more than a handful of dependencies in our projects, it really makes a difference.

The `package.json` file also allows us to *pin* dependencies to certain versions, i.e., we can define a version number for every dependency, which ensures that NPM won't pull the latest version automatically, but exactly the version of a package we need:

```
{
    "dependencies": {
      "request": "2.27.0"
    }
}
```

In this case, NPM will always pull `request` version `2.27.0` (and the dependencies of this version), even if newer versions are available.

Patterns are possible, too:

```
{
    "dependencies": {
      "request": "2.27.x"
    }
}
```

The `x` is a placeholder for any number. This way, NPM would pull in `request` version `2.27.0` and `2.27.5`, but not `2.28.0`.

The official documentation at `https://docs.npmjs.com/misc/semver` has more examples of possible dependency definitions.

Please note that the `package.json` file does much more than just defining dependencies. We will dig deeper in the course of this book.
For now, we are prepared to use NPM for resolving the dependencies that arise in our first project – our first test-driven Node.js application.

Downloading the example code
You can download the example code files for this book from your account at
`http://www.packtpub.com`. The code bundle for the book is also hosted on GitHub at
`https://github.com/PacktPublishing/The-Node-Craftsman-Book`

2
Test-driven Node.js
Development

The code examples in *The Node Beginner Book* only described a toy project, and we came away with not writing any tests for it. If writing tests is new for you, and you have not yet worked on software in a test-driven manner, then I invite you to follow along and give it a try.

We need to decide on a test framework that we will use to implement our tests. A lack of choice is not an issue in the JavaScript and Node.js world, as there are dozens of frameworks available. Personally, I prefer *Jasmine*, and will therefore use it for my examples.

Jasmine is a framework that follows the philosophy of *behaviour-driven development*, which is kind of a *subculture* within the community of test-driven developers. This topic alone could easily fill its own book, thus I'll give only a brief introduction.

The idea is to begin development of a new software unit with its specification, followed by its implementation (which, by definition, must satisfy the specification).

Let's make up a real world example: we order a table from a carpenter. We do so by *specifying* the end result:

I need a table with a top that is 6 x 3 ft. The height of the top must be adjustable—2.5 to 4.0 ft. I want to be able to adjust the top's height without standing up from my chair. I want the table to be black, and cleaning it with a wet cloth should be possible without damaging the material. My budget is $500.

Such a specification allows to share a goal between us and the carpenter. We don't have to care for how exactly the carpenter will achieve this goal. As long as the delivered product fits our specification, both of us can agree that the goal has been reached.

With a test-driven or behaviour-driven approach, this idea is applied to building software. You wouldn't build a piece of software and then define what it's supposed to do. You need to know in advance what you expect a unit of software to do. Instead of doing this vaguely and implicitly, a test-driven approach asks you to do the specification exactly and explicitly. Because we work on software, our specification can be software, too: we only need to write functions that check if our unit does what it is expected to do. These check functions are unit tests.

Let's create a software unit which is covered by tests that describe its expected behaviour. In order to actually drive the creation of the code with the tests, let's write the tests first. We then have a clearly defined goal: making the tests pass by implementing code that fulfills the expected behaviour, and nothing else.

In order to do so, we create a new Node.js project with two folders in it:

```
src/
spec/
```

The spec folder is where our test cases go – in Jasmine lingo, these are called specifications, hence spec. The spec folder mirrors the file structure under src, that is, a source file at src/foo.js is mirrored by a specification at spec/fooSpec.js.

Following the tradition, we will test and implement a Hello World code unit. Its expected behaviour is to return a string Hello Joe! if called with Joe as its first and only parameter. This behaviour can be specified by writing a unit test.

To do so, we create a file spec/greetSpec.js, with the following content:

```
'use strict';

var greet = require('../src/greet');

describe('greet', function() {
```

```
it('should greet the given name', function() {
  expect(greet('Joe')).toEqual('Hello Joe!');
});

it('should greet no-one special if no name is given', function() {
  expect(greet()).toEqual('Hello world!');
});

});
```

This is a simple, yet complete specification. It is a programmatical description of the behaviour we expect from a yet-to-be-written function named greet.

The specification says that if the function greet is called with Joe as its first and only parameter, the return value of the function call should be the string Hello Joe!. If we don't supply a name, the greeting should be generic.

As you can see, Jasmine specifications have a two-level structure. The top level of this structure is a describe block, which consists of one or more it blocks.

An it block describes a single expected behaviour of a single unit under test, and a describe block summarizes one or more blocks of expected behaviours, therefore completely specifying all expected behaviours of a unit.

Let's illustrate this with a real-world *unit* described by a Jasmine specification:

```
describe( 'A candle' , function() {
  it( 'should burn when lighted' , function() {
    // ...
  });
  it( 'should grow smaller while burning' , function() {
    // ...
  });
  it( 'should no longer burn when all wax has been burned', function(){
    // ...
  });
  it( 'should go out when no oxygen is
available to it' , function() {
    // ...
  });
});
```

As you can see, a Jasmine specification gives us a structure to fully describe how a given unit should behave.

Not only can we *describe* expected behaviour, we can also *verify* it. This can be done by running the test cases in the specification against the actual implementation.

After all, our Jasmine specification is just another piece of JavaScript code which can be executed. The NPM package `jasmine-node` ships with a test case runner which allows us to execute the test case, with the added benefit of a nice progress and result output.

Let's create a `package.json` file that defines `jasmine-node` as a dependency of our application – then we can start running the test cases of our specification.

As described earlier, we need to place the `package.json` file at the topmost folder of our project. Its content should be as follows:

```
{
  "devDependencies":  {
    "jasmine-node": "^1.14.5"
  }
}
```

We talked about the `dependencies` section of `package.json` before – but here we declare `jasmine-node` in a `devDependencies` block. The result is basically the same: NPM knows about this dependency and installs the package and its dependencies for us. However, dev dependencies are not needed to run our application – as the name suggests, they are only needed during development.

NPM allows you to skip dev dependencies when deploying applications to a production system – we will get to this later.

In order to have NPM install `jasmine-node`, please run the `npm install` command in the top folder of your project.

We are now ready to test our application against its specification.

Of course, our `greet` function cannot fulfill its specification yet, simply because we have not yet implemented it. Let's see how this looks by running the test cases. From the root folder of our new project, execute the following:

```
./node_modules/jasmine-node/bin/jasmine-node  spec/greetSpec.js
```

As you can see, Jasmine isn't too happy with the results yet. We refer to a Node module in `src/greet.js`, a file that doesn't even exist, which is why Jasmine bails out before even starting the tests:

```
Exception loading: spec/greetSpec.js
{ [Error: Cannot find module '../src/greet'] code: 'MODULE_NOT_FOUND' }
```

Well, let's create the module, in file `src/greet.js`:

```
'use strict' ;

var greet = function() {};

module.exports = greet;
```

Now we have a general infrastructure, but of course we do not yet behave as the specification wishes. Let's run the test cases again:

```
FF
Failures:

  1) greet should greet the given name
   Message:
     TypeError: object is not a function
   Stacktrace:
     TypeError: object is not a function
    at null.<anonymous> (./spec/greetSpec.js:8:12)

  2) greet should greet no-one special if no name is given
   Message:
     TypeError: object is not a function
   Stacktrace:
     TypeError: object is not a function
    at null.<anonymous> (./spec/greetSpec.js:12:12)

Finished in 0.015 seconds
2 tests, 2 assertions, 2 failures, 0 skipped
```

Jasmine tells us that it executed two test cases that contained a total of two assertions (or expectations), and because these expectations could not be satisfied, the test run ended with two failures.

It's time to satisfy the first expectation of our specification, in file `src/greet.js`:

```
'use strict';

var greet = function(name) {
  return 'Hello ' + name + '!';
};

module.exports = greet;
```

Another test case run reveals that we are getting closer:

```
.F
Failures:

  1) greet should greet no-one special if no name is given
   Message:
     Expected 'Hello undefined!' to equal 'Hello world!'.
   Stacktrace:
     Error: Expected 'Hello undefined!' to equal 'Hello world!'.
    at null.<anonymous> (spec/greetSpec.js:12:21)

Finished in 0.015 seconds
2 tests, 2 assertions, 1 failure, 0 skipped
```

Our first test case passes – greet can now correctly greet people by name. We still need to handle the case where no name was given:

```
'use strict';

var greet = function(name) {
  if (name === undefined) {
    name = 'world';
  }
  return 'Hello ' + name + '!';
};
module.exports = greet;
```

And that does the job:

```
..
Finished in 0.007 seconds
2 tests, 2 assertions, 0 failures, 0 skipped
```

We have now created a piece of software that behaves according to its specification.

You'll probably agree that our approach to create this unbelievably complex unit of software – the greet function – in a test-driven way doesn't prove the greatness of test-driven development in any way. That's not the goal of this chapter. It merely sets the stage for what's to come. We are going to create real, comprehensive software through the course of this book, and this is where the advantages of a test-driven approach can be experienced.

3
Object-oriented JavaScript

Let's talk about object-orientation and inheritance in JavaScript.

The good news is that it's actually quite simple, but the bad news is that it works completely different than object-orientation in languages like C++, Java, Ruby, Python or PHP, making it not-quite-so simple to understand.

But fear not, we are going to take it step by step.

Blueprints versus finger-pointing

Let's start by looking at how *typical* object-oriented languages actually create objects.

We are going to talk about an object called `myCar`. The `myCar` object is our bits-and-bytes representation of an incredibly simplified real world car. It could have attributes like `color` and `weight`, and methods like `drive` and `honk`.

In a real application, `myCar` could be used to represent the car in a racing game – but we are going to completely ignore the context of this object, because we will talk about the nature and usage of this object in a more abstract way.

If you would want to use this `myCar` object in, say, Java, you need to define the blueprint of this specific object first – this is what Java and most other object-oriented languages call a **class**.

If you want to create the object `myCar`, you tell Java to *build a new object after the specification that is laid out in the class* `Car`.

The newly built object shares certain aspects with its blueprint. If you call the method `honk` on your object, like so:

```
myCar.honk();
```

Then the Java VM will go to the class of `myCar` and look up which code it actually needs to execute, which is defined in the `honk` method of class `Car`.

Ok, nothing shockingly new here. Enter JavaScript.

A classless society

JavaScript does not have classes. But as in other languages, we would like to tell the interpreter that it should build our `myCar` object following a certain pattern or schema or blueprint – it would be quite tedious to create every `car` object from scratch, *manually* giving it the attributes and methods it needs every time we build it.

If we were to create 30 `car` objects based on the `Car` class in Java, this object-class relationship provides us with 30 cars that are able to drive and honk without us having to write 30 `drive` and `honk` methods.

How is this achieved in JavaScript? Instead of an object-class relationship, there is an object-object relationship.

Where in Java our `myCar`, asked to `honk`, says *go look at this class over there, which is my blueprint, to find the code you need*, JavaScript says *go look at that other object over there, which is my prototype, it has the code you are looking for*.

Building objects via an object-object relationship is called **prototype-based programming**, versus **class-based programming** used in more traditional languages like Java.

Both are perfectly valid implementations of the object-oriented programming paradigm – it's just two different approaches.

Creating objects

Let's dive into code a bit, shall we? How could we set up our code in order to allow us to create our `myCar` object, ending up with an object that is a `Car` and can therefore *honk* and *drive*?

Well, in the most simple sense, we can create our object completely from scratch, or ex nihilo if you prefer the boaster expression.

It works like this:

```
var myCar = {};

myCar.honk = function() {
  console.log('honk honk');
};

myCar.drive = function() {
  console.log('vrooom...');
};
```

This gives us an object called `myCar` that is able to *honk* and *drive:*

```
myCar.honk(); // outputs "honk honk"
myCar.drive(); // outputs "vrooom..."
```

However, if we were to create 30 cars this way, we would end up defining the *honk* and *drive* behaviour of every single one, something we said we want to avoid.

In real life, if we made a living out of creating, say, pencils, and we don't want to create every pencil individually by hand, then we would consider building a pencil-making machine, and have this machine create the pencils for us.

After all, that's what we implicitly do in a class-based language like Java – by defining a class `Car`, we get the car-maker for free:

```
Car myCar = new Car();
```

will build the `myCar` object for us based on the `Car` blueprint. Using the `new` keyword does all the magic for us:

JavaScript, however, leaves the responsibility of building an object creator to us. Furthermore, it gives us a lot of freedom regarding the way we actually build our objects.

In the most simple case, we can write a function which creates plain objects that are exactly like our ex nihilo object, and that don't really share any behaviour – they just happen to roll out of the factory with the same behaviour copied onto every single one, if you want so.

Or, we can write a special kind of function that not only creates our objects, but also does some behind-the-scenes magic which links the created objects with their creator. This allows for a true sharing of behaviour: functions that are available on all created objects point to a single implementation. If this function implementation changes after objects have been created, which is possible in JavaScript, the behaviour of all objects sharing the function will change accordingly.

Let's examine all possible ways of creating objects in detail.

Using a simple function to create plain objects

In our first example, we created a plain `myCar` object out of thin air – we can simply wrap the creation code into a function, which gives us a very basic object creator:

```
var makeCar = function() {
  var newCar = {};
  newCar.honk = function() {
    console.log('honk honk');
  };
};
```

For the sake of brevity, the `drive` function has been omitted.

We can then use this function to mass-produce cars:

```
var makeCar = function() {
  var newCar = {}
  newCar.honk = function() {
    console.log('honk honk');
  };
  return newCar;
};

myCar1 = makeCar();
myCar2 = makeCar();
myCar3 = makeCar();
```

One downside of this approach is efficiency: for every `myCar` object that is created, a new `honk` function is created and attached – creating 1,000 objects means that the JavaScript interpreter has to allocate memory for 1,000 functions, although they all implement the same behaviour. This results in an unnecessarily high memory footprint of the application.

Secondly, this approach deprives us of some interesting opportunities. These `myCar` objects don't share anything – they were built by the same creator function, but are completely independent from each other.

It's really like with real cars from a real car factory: They all look the same, but once they leave the assembly line, they are totally independent. If the manufacturer should decide that pushing the horn on already produced cars should result in a different type of honk, all cars would have to be returned to the factory and modified.

In the virtual universe of JavaScript, we are not bound to such limits. By creating objects in a more sophisticated way, we are able to magically change the behaviour of all created objects at once.

Using a constructor function to create objects

In JavaScript, the entities that create objects with shared behaviour are functions which are called in a special way. These special functions are called **constructors**.

Let's create a constructor for cars. We are going to call this function `Car`, with a capital `C`, which is common practice to indicate that this function is a constructor.

In a way, this makes the constructor function a class, because it does some of the things a class (with a constructor method) does in a traditional OOP language. However, the approach is not identical, which is why constructor functions are often called **pseudo-classes** in JavaScript. I will simply call them classes or constructor functions.

Because we are going to encounter two new concepts that are both necessary for shared object behaviour to work, we are going to approach the final solution in two steps.

Step one is to recreate the previous solution (where a common function spilled out independent car objects), but this time using a constructor:

```
var Car = function() {
  this.honk = function() {
    console.log('honk honk');
  };
};
```

When this function is called using the `new` keyword, like so:

```
var myCar = new Car();
```

It implicitly returns a newly created object with the honk function attached.

Using this and new makes the explicit creation and return of the new object unnecessary - it is created and returned *behind the scenes* (i.e., the new keyword is what creates the new, *invisible* object, and secretly passes it to the Car function as its this variable).

You can think of the mechanism at work a bit like in this pseudo-code:

```
// Pseudo-code, for illustration only!

var Car = function(this) {
  this.honk = function() {
    console.log('honk honk');
  };
  return this;
};

var newObject = {};
var myCar = Car(newObject);
```

As said, this is more or less like our previous solution – we don't have to create every car object manually, but we still cannot modify the *honk* behaviour only once and have this change reflected in all created cars.

But we laid the first cornerstone for it. By using a constructor, all objects received a special property that links them to their constructor:

```
var Car = function() {
  this.honk = function() {
    console.log('honk honk');
  };
};
var myCar1 = new Car();
var myCar2 = new Car();

console.log(myCar1.constructor);   // outputs [Function: Car]
console.log(myCar2.constructor);   // outputs [Function: Car]
```

All created myCars are linked to the Car constructor. This is what actually makes them a *class* of related objects, and not just a bunch of objects that happen to have similar names and identical functions.

Now we have finally reached the moment to get back to the mysterious prototype we talked about in the introduction.

Using prototyping to efficiently share behaviour between objects

As stated there, while in class-based programming the class is the place to put functions that all objects will share, in prototype-based programming, the place to put these functions is the object which acts as the prototype for our objects at hand.

But where is the object that is the prototype of our `myCar` objects – we didn't create one!

It has been implicitly created for us, and is assigned to the `Car.prototype` property (in case you wondered, JavaScript functions are objects too, and they therefore have properties).

Here is the key to sharing functions between objects: Whenever we call a function on an object, the JavaScript interpreter tries to find that function within the queried object. But if it doesn't find the function within the object itself, it asks the object for the pointer to its prototype, then goes to the prototype, and asks for the function there. If it is found, it is then executed.

This means that we can create `myCar` objects without any functions, create the `honk` function in their prototype, and end up having `myCar` objects that know how to honk – because every time the interpreter tries to execute the `honk` function on one of the `myCar` objects, it will be redirected to the prototype, and execute the `honk` function which is defined there.

Here is how this setup can be achieved:

```
var Car = function() {};

Car.prototype.honk = function() {
  console.log('honk honk');
};

var myCar1 = new Car();
var myCar2 = new Car();

myCar1.honk();  // executes Car.prototype.honk() and outputs "honk honk"
myCar2.honk();  // executes Car.prototype.honk() and outputs "honk honk"
```

Our constructor is now empty, because for our very simple cars, no additional setup is necessary.

Because both `myCars` are created through this constructor, their prototype points to `Car.prototype` – executing `myCar1.honk()` and `myCar2.honk()` always results in `Car.prototype.honk()` being executed.

Let's see what this enables us to do. In JavaScript, objects can be changed at runtime. This holds true for prototypes, too. Which is why we can change the `honk` behaviour of all our cars even after they have been created:

```
var Car = function() {};

Car.prototype.honk = function() {
  console.log('honk honk');
};

var myCar1 = new Car();
var myCar2 = new Car();

myCar1.honk();   // executes Car.prototype.honk() and outputs "honk honk"
myCar2.honk();   // executes Car.prototype.honk() and outputs "honk honk"

Car.prototype.honk = function() {
  console.log('meep meep');
};

myCar1.honk();   // executes Car.prototype.honk() and outputs "meep meep"
myCar2.honk();   // executes Car.prototype.honk() and outputs "meep meep"
```

Of course, we can also add additional functions at runtime:

```
var Car = function() {};

Car.prototype.honk = function() {
  console.log('honk honk');
};

var myCar1 = new Car();
var myCar2 = new Car();

Car.prototype.drive = function() {
  console.log('vrooom...');
};

myCar1.drive();   // executes Car.prototype.drive() and outputs "vrooom..."
myCar2.drive();   // executes Car.prototype.drive() and outputs "vrooom..."
```

But we could even decide to treat only one of our cars differently:

```
var Car = function() {};

Car.prototype.honk = function() {
  console.log('honk honk');
};

var myCar1 = new Car();
var myCar2 = new Car();

myCar1.honk();   // executes Car.prototype.honk() and outputs "honk honk"
myCar2.honk();   // executes Car.prototype.honk() and outputs "honk honk"

myCar2.honk = function() {
  console.log('meep meep');
};

myCar1.honk();   // executes Car.prototype.honk() and outputs "honk honk"
myCar2.honk();   // executes myCar2.honk() and outputs "meep meep"
```

It's important to understand what happens behind the scenes in this example. As we have seen, when calling a function on an object, the interpreter follows a certain path to find the actual location of that function.

While for myCar1, there still is no honk function within that object itself, that no longer holds true for myCar2. When the interpreter calls myCar2.honk(), there now is a function within myCar2 itself. Therefore, the interpreter no longer follows the path to the prototype of myCar2, and executes the function within myCar2 instead.

That's one of the major differences to class-based programming: while objects are relatively *rigid* for example, in Java, where the structure of an object cannot be changed at runtime, in JavaScript, the prototype-based approach links objects of a certain class more loosely together, which allows to change the structure of objects at any time.

Also, note how sharing functions through the constructor's prototype is way more efficient than creating objects that all carry their own functions, even if they are identical. As previously stated, the engine doesn't know that these functions are meant to be identical, and it has to allocate memory for every function in every object. This is no longer true when sharing functions through a common prototype – the function in question is placed in memory exactly once, and no matter how many `myCar` objects we create, they don't carry the function themselves, they only refer to their constructor, in whose prototype the function is found.

To give you an idea of what this difference can mean, here is a very simple comparison. The first example creates 1,000,000 objects that all have the function directly attached to them:

```
var C = function() {
  this.f = function(foo) {
    console.log(foo);
  };
};

var a = [];
for (var i = 0; i < 1000000; i++) {
  a.push(new C());
}
```

In Google Chrome, this results in a heap snapshot size of 328 MB. Here is the same example, but now the function is shared through the constructor's prototype:

```
var C = function() {};
C.prototype.f = function(foo) {
  console.log(foo);
};

var a = [];
for (var i = 0; i < 1000000; i++) {
  a.push(new C());
}
```

This time, the size of the heap snapshot is only 17 MB, that is, only about 5% of the non-efficient solution.

Object-orientation, prototyping, and inheritance

So far, we haven't talked about inheritance in JavaScript, so let's do this now.

It's useful to share behaviour within a certain class of objects, but there are cases where we would like to share behaviour between different, but similar classes of objects.

Imagine our virtual world not only had cars, but also bikes. Both drive, but where a car has a horn, a bike has a bell.

Being able to drive makes both objects vehicles, but not sharing the *honk* and *ring* behaviour distinguishes them.

We could illustrate their shared and local behaviour as well as their relationship to each other as follows:

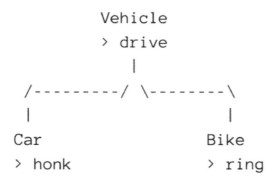

Designing this relationship in a class-based language like Java is straightforward: We would define a class `Vehicle` with a method `drive`, and two classes `Car` and `Bike` which both extend the `Vehicle` class, and implement a `honk` and a `ring` method, respectively.

This would make the `car` as well as `bike` objects inherit the `drive` behaviour through the inheritance of their classes.

How does this work in JavaScript, where we don't have classes, but prototypes?

Let's look at an example first, and then dissect it. To keep the code short for now, let's only start with a car that inherits from a vehicle:

```javascript
var Vehicle = function() {};

Vehicle.prototype.drive = function() {
  console.log('vrooom...');
};


var Car = function() {};

Car.prototype = new Vehicle();

Car.prototype.honk = function() {
  console.log('honk honk');
};


var myCar = new Car();

myCar.honk();    // outputs "honk honk"
myCar.drive();   // outputs "vrooom..."
```

In JavaScript, inheritance runs through a chain of prototypes.

The prototype of the Car constructor is set to a newly created vehicle object, which establishes the link structure that allows the interpreter to look for methods in *parent* objects.

The prototype of the Vehicle constructor has a function drive. Here is what happens when the myCar object is asked to drive():

- The interpreter looks for a drive method within the myCar object, which does not exist
- The interpreter then asks the myCar object for its prototype, which is the prototype of its constructor Car
- When looking at Car.prototype, the interpreter sees a vehicle object which has a function honk attached, but no drive function
- Thus, the interpreter now asks this vehicle object for its prototype, which is the prototype of its constructor Vehicle

- When looking at `Vehicle.prototype`, the interpreter sees an object which has a `drive` function attached – the interpreter now knows which code implements the `myCar.drive()` behaviour, and executes it

A classless society, revisited

We just learned how to emulate the traditional OOP inheritance mechanism. But it's important to note that in JavaScript, that is only one valid approach to create objects that are related to each other.

It was Douglas Crockford who came up with another clever solution, which allows objects to inherit from each other directly. It's a native part of JavaScript by now – it's the `Object.create()` function, and it works like this:

```
Object.create = function(o) {
  var F = function() {};
  F.prototype = o;
  return new F();
};
```

We learned enough now to understand what's going on. Let's analyze an example:

```
var vehicle = {};
vehicle.drive = function () {
  console.log('vrooom...');
};

var car = Object.create(vehicle);
car.honk = function() {
  console.log('honk honk');
};

var myCar = Object.create(car);

myCar.honk();   // outputs "honk honk"
myCar.drive();  // outputs "vrooom..."
```

While being more concise and expressive, this code achieves exactly the same behaviour, without the need to write dedicated constructors and attaching functions to their prototype. As you can see, `Object.create()` handles both behind the scenes, on the fly. A temporary constructor is created, its prototype is set to the object that serves as the role model for our new object, and a new object is created from this setup.

Conceptually, this is really the same as in the previous example where we defined that `Car.prototype` shall be a `new Vehicle();`.

But wait! We created the functions `drive` and `honk` within our objects, not on their prototypes –that's memory-inefficient!

Well, in this case, it's actually not. Let's see why:

```
var vehicle = {};
vehicle.drive = function () {
  console.log('vrooom...');
};

var car = Object.create(vehicle);
car.honk = function() {
  console.log('honk honk');
};

var myVehicle = Object.create(vehicle);
var myCar1 = Object.create(car);
var myCar2 = Object.create(car);

myCar1.honk();   // outputs "honk honk"
myCar2.honk();   // outputs "honk honk"

myVehicle.drive();   // outputs "vrooom..."
myCar1.drive();   // outputs "vrooom..."
myCar2.drive();   // outputs "vrooom..."
```

We have now created a total of 5 objects, but how often do the `honk` and `drive` methods exist in memory? Well, how often have they been defined? Just once – and therefore, this solution is basically as efficient as the one where we built the inheritance manually. Let's look at the numbers:

```
var c = {};
c.f = function(foo) {
  console.log(foo);
};

var a = [];
for (var i = 0; i < 1000000; i++) {
  a.push(Object.create(c));
}
```

Turns out, it's not *exactly* identical – we end up with a heap snapshot size of 40 MB, thus there seems to be some overhead involved. However, in exchange for much better code, this is probably more than worth it.

Summary

By now, it's probably clear what the main difference between classical OOP languages and JavaScript is, conceptually: While classical languages like Java provide *one* way to manage object creation and behaviour sharing (through classes and inheritance), and this way is enforced by the language and *baked in*, JavaScript starts at a slightly lower level and provides building blocks that allow us to create several different mechanisms for this.

Whether you decide to use these building blocks to recreate the traditional class-based pattern, let your objects inherit from each other directly, with the concept of classes getting in the way, or if you don't use the object-oriented paradigm at all and just solve the problem at hand with pure functional code: JavaScript gives you the freedom to choose the best methodology for any situation.

4
Synchronous and Asynchronous Operations Explained

Visualizing the Node.js execution model

For the chapters that follow it's important to fully understand what it means, conceptually, that a Node.js application has synchronous and asynchronous operations, and how both operations interact with each other.

Let's try to build this understanding step by step.

The first concept that we need to understand is that of the Node.js event loop. The event loop is the execution model of a running Node.js application.

We can visualize this model as a row of loops:

```
+----> -----+   +----> -----+   +----> -----+   +----> -----+
|           |   |           |   |           |   |           |
|           |   |           |   |           |   |           |
|           |   |           |   |           |   |           |
|           |   |           |   |           |   |           |
|           |   |           |   |           |   |           |
+-----------+   +-----------+   +-----------+   +-----------+
```

I've drawn boxes because circles look really clumsy in ASCII art. So, these here look like rectangles, but please imagine them as circles - circles with an arrow, which means that one circle represents one iteration through the event loop.

Another visualization could be the following pseudo-code:

```
while (I still have stuff to do) {
  do stuff;
}
```

Conceptually, at the very core of it, it's really that simple: Node.js starts, loads our application, and then loops until there is nothing left to do – at which point our application terminates.

What kind of stuff is happening inside one loop iteration? Let's first look at a very simple example, a Hello World application like this:

```
console.log('Hello');
console.log('World');
```

This is the visualization of the execution of this application in our ASCII art:

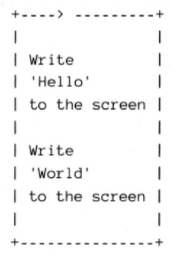

Yep, that's it: Just one iteration, and then, exit the application.

The things we asked our application to do – writing text to the screen, and then writing another text to the screen, using `console.log` – are *synchronous* operations. They both happen within the same (and in this case, only) iteration through the event loop.

Let's look at the model when we bring asynchronous operations into the game, like this:

```
console.log('Hello');
setTimeout(function() {
  console.log('World');
}, 1000);
```

This still prints Hello and then World to the screen, but the second text is printed with a delay of 1000 ms.

The setTimeout function, you may have guessed it, is an *asynchronous* operation. We pass the code to be executed in the body of an anonymous function – the so-called **callback function**. Why do we do so? The visualization helps to understand why:

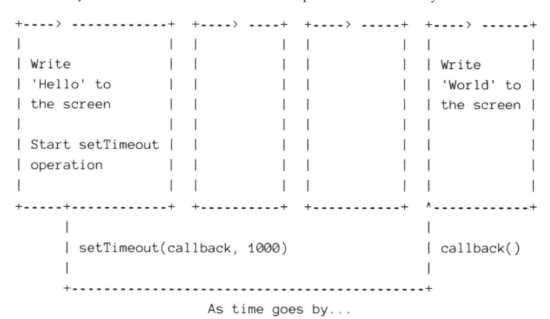

This, again at the very core of it, is what calling an asynchronous function does: It starts an operation *outside the event loop*. Conceptually, Node.js starts the asynchronous operation and makes a mental note that when this operations triggers an event, the anonymous function that was passed to the operation needs to be called.

Hence, the *event loop*: as long as asynchronous operations are ongoing, the Node.js process loops, waiting for events from those operations. As soon as no more asynchronous operations are ongoing, the looping stops and our application terminates.

The visualization isn't detailed enough to show that Node.js checks for outside events *between* loop iterations.

Just to be clear: callback functions don't need to be anonymous inline functions:

```
var write_world = function() {
  console.log('World');
};
console.log('Hello');

setTimeout(write_world, 1000);
```

The preceding code results in:

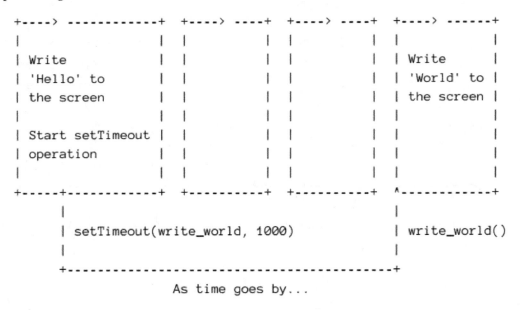

It's just that more often than not, declaring a named function and passing it as the callback isn't worth the hassle, because very often we need the functionality described in the function only once.

Let's look at a slightly more interesting asynchronous operation, the `fs.stat` call – it starts an IO operation that looks at the file system information for a given path, that is, stuff like the inode number, the size and so on:

```
var fs = require('fs');
fs.stat('/etc/passwd', function(err, stats) {
  console.dir(stats);
});
```

The visualization:

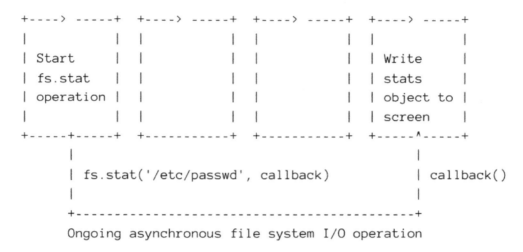

```
+----> -----+  +----> -----+  +----> -----+  +----> -----+
|          |  |          |  |          |  |          |
| Start    |  |          |  |          |  | Write    |
| fs.stat  |  |          |  |          |  | stats    |
| operation|  |          |  |          |  | object to|
|          |  |          |  |          |  | screen   |
+-----+-----+  +----------+  +----------+  +-----^-----+
      |                                          |
      | fs.stat('/etc/passwd', callback)         | callback()
      |                                          |
      +-------------------------------------------+
       Ongoing asynchronous file system I/O operation
```

Really not that different – instead of Node.js merely counting milliseconds in the background, it starts an IO operation; IO operations are expensive, and several loop iterations go by where nothing happens. Then, Node.js has finished the background IO operation, and triggers the callback we passed in order to jump back – right into the current loop iteration. We then print – very synchronously – the `stats` object to the screen.

Another classical example: When we start an HTTP server, we create a background operation which continuously waits for HTTP requests from clients:

```
var http = require('http');
http.createServer(function(request, response) {
  response.writeHead(200, {'Content-Type': 'text/html'});
  response.write('<b>Hello World</b>');
  response.end();
}).listen(8080);
```

Whenever this event occurs, the passed callback is triggered:

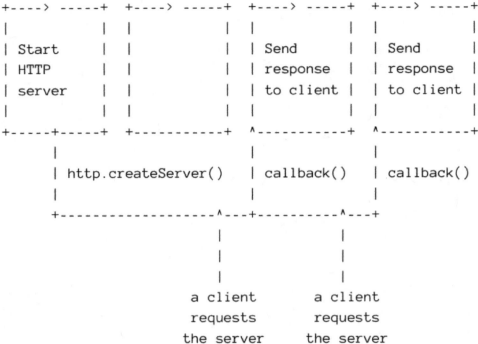

Blocking and non-blocking operations

From the understanding of this conceptual model, we can get to understanding the difference between blocking and non-blocking operations.

The key to understanding these is the realization that *every* synchronous operation results in a blocking operation. That's right, even an innocent `console.log('Hello World');` results in a blocking operation – while the Node.js process writes the text to the screen, this is the *only* thing that it does. There is only one single piece of JavaScript code that can be executed within the event loop at any given time.

The reason this doesn't result in a problem in the case of a `console.log()` is that it is an extremely cheap operation. In comparison, even the most simple IO operations are way more expensive. Whenever the network or hard drives (yes, including SSDs) are involved, expect things to be *incredibly much slower* compared to operations where only the CPU and RAM are involved, like `var a = 2 * 21`. Just how much slower? The following table gives you a good idea – it shows actual times for different kind of computer operations, and shows how they relate to each other compared to how time spans that human beings experience relate to each other:

```
1 CPU cycle                       0.3 ns        1 s
Level 1 cache access              0.9 ns        3 s
Level 2 cache access              2.8 ns        9 s
Level 3 cache access             12.9 ns       43 s
Main memory access                120 ns        6 min
Solid-state disk I/O           50-150 μs     2-6 days
Rotational disk I/O              1-10 ms    1-12 months
Internet: SF to NYC                40 ms        4 years
Internet: SF to UK                 81 ms        8 years
Internet: SF to Australia         183 ms       19 years
OS virtualization reboot            4 s       423 years
SCSI command time-out              30 s      3000 years
Hardware virtualization reboot     40 s      4000 years
Physical system reboot              5 m       32 millenia
```

So, the difference between setting a variable in your code and reading even a tiny file from disk is like the difference between preparing a sandwich and going on vacation for a week. You can prepare a lot of sandwiches during one week of vacation.

And that's the sole reason why all those Node.js functions that result in IO operations also happen to work asynchronously: it's because the event loop needs being kept free of any long-running operations during which the Node.js process would practically stall, which would result in unresponsive applications.

Just to be clear: we can easily stall the event loop even if no IO operations are involved and we only use cheap synchronous functions – if only there are enough of them within one loop iteration. Take the following code for example:

```
var http = require('http');

http.createServer(function(request, response) {
    console.log('Handling HTTP request');
```

```
    response.writeHead(200, {'Content-Type': 'text/html'});
    response.write('<b>Hello World</b>');
    response.end();
}).listen(8080);

var a;
for (var i=0; i < 10000000000; i += 1) {
  a = i;
}

console.log('For loop has finished');
```

It's our minimalistic web server again, plus a for loop with 10,000,000,000 iterations.

Our event loop visualization basically looks the same:

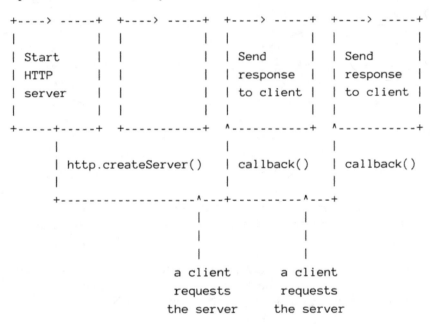

But here is the problem: The HTTP server will start listening in the background as an asynchronous operation, but we will stay within the first loop operation as long as the `for` loop is running. And although we only have a very cheap operation happening within the for loop, it happens 10,000,000,000 times, and on my machine, this takes around 20 seconds.

When you start the server application and then open your browser at http://localhost:8080/, you won't get an answer right away. External events, like our HTTP request, are only handled between one loop iteration and the next; however, the first loop iteration takes 20 seconds because of our `for` loop, and only then Node.js switches to the next iteration and has a chance to handle our request by calling the HTTP server callback.

As you will see, the application will print **For loop has finished**, and right after that, it will answer the HTTP request and print **Handling HTTP request**. This demonstrates how external events from asynchronous operations are handled at the beginning of a new event loop iteration.

You've probably heard time and again how Node.js isn't suited for writing applications with CPU intensive tasks - as we can see, the reason for this is the event loop model.

From this, we can distill the two most important rules for writing responsive Node.js applications:

- Handle IO-intensive operations through asynchronous operations
- Keep your own code (that is, everything that happens synchronously within event loop iterations) as lean as possible

This leaves the question: what are sensible solutions if you *have* to do expensive CPU-bound operations within your JavaScript code? As we will learn in later chapters, we can mitigate the problem that Node.js itself simply isn't particularly suited for these kinds of operations.

5
Using and Creating Event Emitters

Introduction

By now, you are probably more than familiar with this:

```
someFunction(function(err) {
  if (!err) {
    console.log('Hey, looks like someFunction has finished and called
    me.');
  } else {
    console.log('Oh no, something terrible happened!');
  }
});
```

We call a function, `someFunction` in this case, which does something asynchronously in the background, and calls the anonymous function we passed in (the *callback*) once it has finished, passing an *Error* object if something went wrong, or *null* if all went fine. That's the standard callback pattern, and you will encounter it regularly when writing Node.js code.

For simple use cases, where we call a function that finishes its task some time in the future, either successfully or with an error, this pattern is just fine.

For more complex use cases, this pattern does not scale well. There are cases where we call a function which results in multiple events happening over time, and also, different types of events might happen.

One example is reading the contents of a file through a `ReadStream`. The details of handling files are discussed in a later chapter, but we will use this example to illustrate event emitters.

This snippet demonstrates how to read data from a large file using a `ReadStream`:

```
'use strict';

var fs = require('fs');

fs.createReadStream('/path/to/large/file');
```

When reading data from a file, two different things can happen: We either receive content, or we reach the end of the file. Both cases *could* be handled using the callback pattern – for example, by using one callback with two parameters, one with the data and another one that is *false* as long as the end of the file has not been reached, and *true* once it has been reached. Or we could provide two separate callback functions, one that is called when content is retrieved and one that is called when the end of the file has been reached.

But there is a more elegant way. Instead of working with classical callbacks, `createReadStream` allows us to use an *event emitter*. That's a special object which can be used to attach callback functions to different events. Using it looks like this:

```
'use strict';

var fs = require('fs');

var stream = fs.createReadStream('/path/to/large/file');

stream.on('data', function(data) {
  console.log('Received data: ' + data);
});

stream.on('end', function() {
  console.log('End of file has been reached');
});
```

Here is what happens in detail:

- In the `var stream = fs.createReadStream('/path/to/large/file');` line, we create a read stream that will start to retrieve the contents of the `/path/to/large/file` file. The call to `fs.createReadStream` does not take a function argument to use it as a callback. Instead, it returns an object, which we assign as the value of the `stream` variable.
- In the `stream.on('data', function(data) {` line, we attach a callback to one type of events `ReadStream` emits: `data` events.
- In the `stream.on('end', function() {` line, we attach another callback to another type of event `ReadStream` emits: the `end` event.

The object that is returned by `fs.createReadStream` is an *event emitter*. These objects allow us to attach different callbacks to different events while keeping our code readable and sane.

A `ReadStream` retrieves the contents of a file in chunks, which is more efficient than to load the whole data of potentially huge files into memory at once in one long, blocking operation.

Because of this, the `data` event will be emitted multiple times, depending on the size of the file. The callback that is attached to this event will therefore be called multiple times.

When all content has been retrieved, the `end` event is fired once, and no other events will be fired from then on. The `end` event callback is therefore the right place to do whatever we want to do after we retrieved the complete file content. In practice, this would look like this:

```
'use strict';

var fs = require('fs');

var stream = fs.createReadStream('/path/to/large/file');

var content = '';

stream.on('data', function(data) {
  content = content + data;
});

stream.on('end', function() {
  console.log('File content has been retrieved: ' + content);
});
```

It doesn't make too much sense to efficiently read a large file's content in chunks, only to assign the whole data to a variable and therefore using the memory anyways. In a real application, we would read a file in chunks to, for example, send every chunk to a web client that is downloading the file via HTTP. We will talk about this in more detail in a later chapter.

The *event emitter* pattern itself is simple and clearly defined: a function returns an event emitter object, and using this object's on method, callbacks can be attached to events.

However, there is no strict rule regarding the events themselves: an event *type*, like data or end, is just a string, and the author of an event emitter can define any name she wants. Also, it's not defined what arguments are passed to the callbacks that are triggered through an event – the author of the event emitter should define this through some kind of documentation.

There is one recurring pattern, at least for the internal Node.js modules, and that is the error event: Most event emitters emit an event called error whenever an error occurs, and if we don't listen to this event, the event emitter will raise an exception.

You can easily test this by running the above code: as long as you don't happen to have a file at /path/to/large/file, Node.js will bail out with this message:

```
events.js:72
        throw er; // Unhandled 'error' event
        ^
Error: ENOENT, open '/path/to/large/file'
```

But if you attach a callback to the error event, you can handle the error yourself:

```
'use strict';

var fs = require('fs');

var stream = fs.createReadStream('/path/to/large/file');

var content = '';

stream.on('error', function(err) {
  console.log('Sad panda: ' + err);
});

stream.on('data', function(data) {
  content = content + data;
});

stream.on('end', function() {
```

```
  console.log('File content has been retrieved: ' + content);
});
```

Instead of using `on`, we can also attach a callback to an event using `once`. Callbacks that are attached this way will be called the first time that the event occurs, but will then be removed from the list of event listeners and not be called again:

```
stream.once('data', function(data) {
  console.log('I have received the first chunk of data');
});
```

Also, it's possible to detach an attached callback manually. This only works with named `callback` functions:

```
var callback = function(data) {
  console.log('I have received a chunk of data: ' + data);
}
stream.on('data', callback);

stream.removeListener('data', callback);
```

And last but not least, you can remove all attached listeners for a certain event:

```
stream.removeAllListeners('data');
```

Creating your own event emitter object

We can create event emitters ourselves. This is even supported by Node.js by inheriting from the built-in `events.EventEmitter` class. But let's first implement a simple event emitter from scratch, because this explains the pattern in all its details.

For this, we are going to create a module whose purpose is to regularly watch for changes in the size of a file. Once implemented, it can be used like this:

```
'use strict';

watcher = new FilesizeWatcher('/path/to/file');

watcher.on('error', function(err) {
  console.log('Error watching file:', err);
});

watcher.on('grew', function(gain) {
  console.log('File grew by', gain, 'bytes');
});
```

```
watcher.on('shrank', function(loss) {
  console.log('File shrank by', loss, 'bytes');
});

watcher.stop();
```

As you can see, the module consists of a class `FilesizeWatcher` which can be instantiated with a file path and returns an event emitter. We can listen to three different events from this emitter: `error`, `grew`, and `shrank`.

Let's start by writing a spec that describes how we expect to use our event emitter. To do so, create a new project directory, and add the following `package.json`:

```
{
  "devDependencies": {
    "jasmine-node": "^1.14.5"
  }
}
```

Afterwards, run `npm install` command.

Now create a file `FilesizeWatcherSpec.js`, with the following content:

```
'use strict';

var FilesizeWatcher = require('./FilesizeWatcher');
var exec = require('child_process').exec;

describe('FilesizeWatcher', function() {

  var watcher;

  afterEach(function() {
    watcher.stop();
  });

  it('should fire a "grew" event when the file grew in size',
  function(done) {

    var path = '/var/tmp/filesizewatcher.test';
    exec('rm -f ' + path + ' ; touch ' + path, function() {
      watcher = new FilesizeWatcher(path);

      watcher.on('grew', function(gain) {
        expect(gain).toBe(5);
        done();
      });
```

```
    exec('echo "test" > ' + path, function() {});

  });

});

it('should fire a "shrank" event when the file grew in size',
function(done) {

  var path = '/var/tmp/filesizewatcher.test';
  exec('rm -f ' + path + ' ; echo "test" > ' + path, function() {
    watcher = new FilesizeWatcher(path);

    watcher.on('shrank', function(loss) {
      expect(loss).toBe(3);
      done();
    });

    exec('echo "a" > ' + path, function() {});

  });

});

it('should fire "error" if path does not start with a slash',
function(done) {

  var path = 'var/tmp/filesizewatcher.test';
  watcher = new FilesizeWatcher(path);

  watcher.on('error', function(err) {
    expect(err).toBe('Path does not start with a slash');
    done();
  });

});

});
```

 Because this is just an example application, we will not create a `spec` and a `src` directory, but instead just put both the specification file and the implementation file in the top folder of our project.

Before we look at the specification itself in detail, let's discuss the done() call we see in each of the it blocks. The done function is a callback that is passed to the function parameter of an it block by Jasmine.

This pattern is used when testing asynchronous operations. Our emitter emits events asynchronously, and Jasmine cannot know by itself when events will fire. It needs our help by being told *now the asynchronous operation I expected to occur* did *actually occur* – and this is done by triggering the callback.

Now to the specification itself. The first expectation is that when we write *test* into our test file, the grew event is fired, telling us that the file gained 5 bytes in size.

Note how we use the exec function from the child_process module to manipulate our test file through shell commands within the specification.

Next, we specify the behaviour that is expected if the monitored test file shrinks in size: the shrank event must fire and report how many bytes the file lost.

At last, we specify that if we ask the watcher to monitor a file path that doesn't start with a slash, an error event must be emitted.

I'm creating a very simplified version of a file size watcher here for the sake of brevity – for a real world implementation, more sophisticated checks would make sense.

We will create two different implementations which both fulfill this specification.

First, we will create a version of the file size watcher where we manage the event listener and event emitting logic completely ourselves. This way, we experience first hand how the event emitter pattern works.

Afterwards, we will implement a second version where we make use of existing Node.js functionality in order to implement the event emitter pattern without the need to reinvent the wheel.

The following shows a possible implementation of the first version, where we take care of the event listener callbacks ourselves:

```
'use strict';

var fs = require('fs');

var FilesizeWatcher = function(path) {
  var self = this;

  self.callbacks = {};

  if (/^\//.test(path) === false) {
    self.callbacks['error']('Path does not start with a slash');
    return;
  }

  fs.stat(path, function(err, stats) {
      self.lastfilesize = stats.size;
  });

  self.interval = setInterval(
    function() {
      fs.stat(path, function(err, stats) {
        if (stats.size > self.lastfilesize) {
          self.callbacks['grew'](stats.size - self.lastfilesize);
          self.lastfilesize = stats.size;
        }
        if (stats.size < self.lastfilesize) {
          self.callbacks['shrank'](self.lastfilesize - stats.size);
          self.lastfilesize = stats.size;
        }
      }, 1000);
    });
};

FilesizeWatcher.prototype.on = function(eventType, callback) {
  this.callbacks[eventType] = callback;
};

FilesizeWatcher.prototype.stop = function() {
  clearInterval(this.interval);
};

module.exports = FilesizeWatcher;
```

Let's discuss this code:

- In the `var fs = require('fs');` line, we load the `fs` module—we need its `stat` function to asynchronously retrieve file information.
- Next, we start to build a constructor function for the `FilesizeWatcher` objects. They are created by passing a path to watch as a parameter.
- We then assign the object instance variable to a local `self` variable—this way we can access our instantiated object within callback functions, where `this` would point to another object.
- We then create the `self.callbacks` object—we are going to use this as an associative array where we will store the callback to each event.
- Next, we check if the given path starts with a slash using a regular expression—if it doesn't, we trigger the callback associated with the `error` event.
- If the check succeeds, we start an initial `stat` operation in order to store the file size of the given path—we need this base value in order to recognize future changes in file size.
- Then the actual watch logic starts at the `self.interval = setInterval(` line. We set up a 1-second interval where we call `stat` on every interval iteration and compare the current file size with the last known file size.
- The `if (stats.size > self.lastfilesize) {` line handles the case where the file grew in size, calling the event handler callback associated with the `grew` event; the `if (stats.size < self.lastfilesize) {` line handles the opposite case. In both cases, the new file size is saved.
- Event handlers can be registered using the `FilesizeWatcher.on` method. In our implementation, all it does is to store the callback under the event name in our `callbacks` object.
- Finally, the `FilesizeWatcher.prototype.stop = function()` `{` line defines the `stop` method, which cancels the interval we set up in the constructor function.

Let's see if this implementation works by running `./node_modules/jasmine-node/bin/jasmine-node ./FilesizeWatcherSpec.js`:

```
..F

Failures:

  1) FilesizeWatcher should fire "error" if the path does not start with a
slash
    Message:
      TypeError: Object #<Object> has no method 'error'
    Stacktrace:
      TypeError: Object #<Object> has no method 'error'
    at new FilesizeWatcher (FilesizeWatcher.js:11:28)
      at null.<anonymous> (FilesizeWatcherSpec.js:51:15)
      at null.<anonymous> (...mine-node/lib/jasmine-node/async-
callback.js:45:37)

Finished in 0.087 seconds
3 tests, 3 assertions, 1 failure, 0 skipped
```

Well... nearly. The core functionality works: the `grew` and `shrank` events are fired as expected.

But the file path check makes problems. According to the message, the problem arises on `self.callbacks[ 'error' ]( 'Path does not start with a slash' );` line.

The error message says that the `self.callbacks` object doesn't have a method called `error`. But in our specification, we defined a callback for this event, just as we did for the other events, in `watcher.on('error', function(err) {` line of `FilesizeWatcherSpec.js`:

The problem here is quite subtle and can only be understood if one remembers how the execution model of Node.js works. Let's recall the chapter on synchronous and asynchronous operations. Our specification code looks like this:

```
watcher = new FilesizeWatcher(path);

watcher.on('error', function(err) {
  expect(err).toBe('Path does not start with a slash');
  done();
});
```

According to the visualization technique we used to explain the inner workings of the event loop model, this is what actually happens:

```
+----> ------+  +----> -----+  +----> -----+  +----> -----+
|           |  |           |  |           |  |           |
| Create    |  |           |  |           |  |           |
| watcher   |  |           |  |           |  |           |
| object    |  |           |  |           |  |           |
|           |  |           |  |           |  |           |
| Check path|  |           |  |           |  |           |
|           |  |           |  |           |  |           |
| Trigger   |  |           |  |           |  |           |
| error     |  |           |  |           |  |           |
| callback  |  |           |  |           |  |           |
|           |  |           |  |           |  |           |
| Attach    |  |           |  |           |  |           |
| callback  |  |           |  |           |  |           |
| to error  |  |           |  |           |  |           |
| event     |  |           |  |           |  |           |
|           |  |           |  |           |  |           |
+-----------+  +-----------+  +-----------+  +-----------+
```

Now it becomes clear that the order in which things are happening is simply wrong: We first call the error callback, and then we attach it. This can't work.

When creating the watcher object, we call the Filesizewatcher constructor function. Up to the point where it checks the path and calls the error event handler callback, everything happens synchronously:

```
var FilesizeWatcher = function(path) {
  var self = this;
  self.callbacks = {};

  if (/^\//.test(path) === false) {
    self.callbacks['error']('Path does not start with a slash');
    return;
  }
```

The constructor function returns and Node.js execution continues with the main code, all the while we are still in the first event loop iteration. Only now - afterwards - we attach the event handler callback for the `error` event; but the constructor already tried to call it!

Why doesn't this problem arise with the `grew` and `shrank` events? Here is the visualization:

```
+----> ------+  +----> -----+  +----> -----+  +----> -----+
|       |    |  |       |   |  |       |   |  |       |    |
| Create |   |  |       |   |  |       |   |  |       |    |
| watcher |  |  |       |   |  |       |   |  |       |    |
| object |   |  |       |   |  |       |   |  |       |    |
|       |    |  |       |   |  |       |   |  |       |    |
| Start |    |  |       |   |  |       |   |  |       |    |
| check |    |  |       |   |  |       |   |  |       |    |
| interval | |  |       |   |  |       |   |  |       |    |
|       |    |  |       |   |  |       |   |  |       |    |
| Attach |   |  |       |   |  |       |   |  |       |    |
| callback | |  |       |   |  |       |   |  |       |    |
| to grew |  |  |       |   |  |       |   |  |       |    |
| event |    |  |       |   |  |       |   |  |       |    |
|       |    |  |       |   |  |       |   |  |       |    |
+-----+------+  +-----------+  +------^-----+  +-----------+
      |                              |
      | setInterval()                | callback()
      |                              |
      +---------------+              |
                      |              |
                      | fs.stat()    |
                      |              |
                      +--------------+
```

This shows how our main code in the first event loop starts the asynchronous `setInterval` operation which in turn starts an asynchronous `stat` operation. Only several event loop iterations later, when the callback for the `grew` event has long been attached, is this callback triggered. No problem arises.

How can we solve the problem for our `error` event? The solution is to put the triggering of the not-yet-attached callback into the future, into the next event loop iteration; this way, the callback will be triggered in the second event loop iteration *after* it has been attached in the first event loop iteration.

Moving code execution into the next event loop iteration is simple thanks to the `process.nextTick` method. Here is how the relevant part in file `FilesizeWatcher.js` needs to be rewritten:

```
if (/^\//.test(path) === false) {
  process.nextTick(function() {
self.callbacks[ 'error' ]( 'Path does not start with a slash' );
  });
  return;
}
```

With this, we put the callback triggering for the `error` event listener into a callback function that will be executed by `process.nextTick` on the next iteration of the event loop:

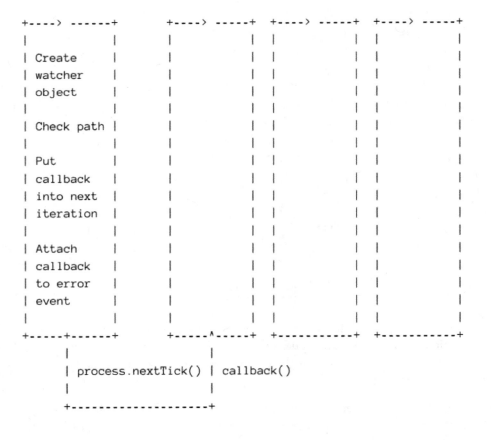

Thus we ensure that it is called *after* it has been defined.

As mentioned, Node.js supports us in creating event emitters, sparing us from writing the callback handling code for our own emitters.

We can use this support by inheriting from an existing class `EventEmitter` in module `events`.

Because the expected behaviour of our *MyEmitter* doesn't change from an outside perspective, we will leave the spec unchanged, and only change our implementation from using a self-made solution to utilizing the existing Node.js class:

```
'use strict';

var fs = require('fs');
var util = require('util');
var EventEmitter = require('events').EventEmitter;

var FilesizeWatcher = function(path) {
  var self = this;

  if (/^\//.test(path) === false) {
    process.nextTick(function() {
      self.emit('error', 'Path does not start with a slash');
    });
    return;
  }

  fs.stat(path, function(err, stats) {
    self.lastfilesize = stats.size;
  });

  self.interval = setInterval(
    function() {
      fs.stat(path, function(err, stats) {
        if (stats.size > self.lastfilesize) {
          self.emit('grew', stats.size - self.lastfilesize);
          self.lastfilesize = stats.size;
        }
        if (stats.size < self.lastfilesize) {
          self.emit('shrank', self.lastfilesize - stats.size);
          self.lastfilesize = stats.size;
        }
      }, 1000);
    });
};
```

```
util.inherits(FilesizeWatcher, EventEmitter);

FilesizeWatcher.prototype.stop = function() {
  clearInterval(this.interval);
};

module.exports = FilesizeWatcher;
```

The interesting part here is `util.inherits(FilesizeWatcher, EventEmitter);` line.

We use a helper function that ships with Node.js, `util.inherits`. We use it to make our `FilesizeWatcher` class a descendant of `events.EventEmitter`, which also ships with Node.js. This class implements all the logic that is needed to act as an event emitter, and our `FilesizeWatcher` class inherits this logic. This way, our own code now concentrates on implementing its specific logic, without having to care about the details of registering callbacks and checking if these can be called and so on.

According to our tests, `FilesizeWatcher` still behaves as it did before:

```
. . .

Finished in 0.052 seconds
3 tests, 3 assertions, 0 failures, 0 skipped
```

Instead of using `util.inherits`, we can also create the inheritance by placing a new `events.EventEmitter` object on the prototype of `FilesizeWatcher`:

```
FilesizeWatcher.prototype = new EventEmitter();
```

Although `util.inherits` adds some extra properties to our constructor, the result is the same, behaviour-wise. Give it a try if you like and see if the tests still pass.

Summary

The asynchronous development style using callbacks that is a recurring pattern in JavaScript and Node.js applications can at times result in a code structure that is hard to understand. Applying the event emitter pattern comes in handy in situations where more than one callback event must be handled, resulting in a cleaner code structure that is easier to follow and reason about. The pattern is so useful that we should use it for our own objects and functions where it makes sense, something that's made easy by utilizing the existing `util.inherits` class.

6
Optimizing Code Performance and Control Flow Management Using the Async Library

Writing or using functions or methods in your code that are executed one after the other gets you a long way in your applications.

Sometimes, those functions are simple synchronous steps:

```
console.log('Starting calculation...');
var result = 5 + 4;
console.log('The result is', result);
```

Often, callbacks are used when operations are executed in the background and jump back into our code's control flow asynchronously at a later point in time:

```
console.log('Starting calculation...');
startExpensiveCalculation(5, 4, function(err, result) {
  if (!err) {
    console.log('The result is', result);
  }
});
```

If those asynchronous background operations bring forth a more complex callback behaviour, they might be implemented as an event emitter:

```
console.log('Starting calculation...');

calculation = Calculator.start(5, 4);

calculation.on('error', function(err) {
```

```
      console.log('An error occured:', err);
    });

    calculation.on('interim result', function(result) {
      console.log('Received interim result:', result);
    });

    calculation.on('done', function(result) {
      console.log('Received final result:', result);
    });
```

Handling expensive operations asynchronously in the background, especially if they are IO-bound, is an important key to making Node.js applications perform efficiently – reading a large file or writing a lot of records to a database will always be a costly procedure, but handling it asynchronously at least ensures that the other parts of our application won't be blocked while that procedure is going on.

Nevertheless, there is often potential for optimization within our own code and its control flow.

Executing expensive asynchronous background tasks in parallel

Let's consider an example where our application queries several different remote web services, presenting the retrieved data on the console.

We are not going to query real remote web services, instead we will write a very simple Node.js HTTP server that will serve as a dummy web service. Our web server doesn't really do anything significant, and therefore we will make it react to requests a bit slower than necessary, in order to simulate a real web service that has a certain workload – as you will see, this makes it easier for us to show the performance gain in our own code optimizations.

Please create a new project folder and create a file server.js with the following content:

```
    'use strict';

    var http = require('http');
    var url = require('url');
    var querystring = require('querystring');

    http.createServer(function(request, response) {

      var pathname = url.parse(request.url).pathname;
```

```
    var query = url.parse(request.url).query;
    var id = querystring.parse(query)['id'];

    var result = {
      'pathname': pathname,
      'id': id,
      'value': Math.floor(Math.random() * 100)
    };

    setTimeout(function() {
      response.writeHead(200, {"Content-Type": "application/json"});
      response.end(JSON.stringify(result));
    }, 2000 + Math.floor(Math.random() * 1000));
}).listen(
  8080,
  function() {
    console.log('Echo Server listening on port 8080');
  }
);
```

This gives us a very simple *echo* server – if we request the URL
`http://localhost:8080/getUser?id=4`, we receive
`{"pathname":"/getUser","id":"4","value":67}` as the response. This is good
enough to give us the simulation of a remote web service API to play around with.

But alas, it's a slow web service! Someone didn't do his optimization homework, and we
now have to deal with an API where every response takes between 2 to 3 seconds (this is
simulated with the `setTimeout` construct).

This allows to show how different request patterns will result in different runtime
characteristics.

We will now write a Node.js client for this web server. This client will make two
consecutive requests to the server, and print the output for both requests on the command
line:

```
'use strict';

var request = require('request');

request.get(
  'http://localhost:8080/getUserName?id=1234',
  function(err, res, body) {
    var result = JSON.parse(body);
    var name = result.value;
```

```
request.get(
  'http://localhost:8080/getUserStatus?id=1234',
  function(err, res, body) {
    var result = JSON.parse(body);
    var status = result.value;

    console.log('The status of user', name, 'is', status);
  });

});
```

 Save this in a file called `client.js`. Also, you need to install the `request` module via `npm install request@2.79.0`.

This is probably the most straight-forward solution. We start the first request, wait for it to finish, print the result, then start the second request, wait for it to finish, and print that result, too.

How long does that take? Let's see:

```
$ time node client.js
The status of user 62 is 68
real    0m5.810s
user    0m0.172s
sys     0m0.033s
```

 Don't forget to start the server via node `server.js` beforehand!

Not surprisingly, it takes around 5-6 seconds, because we only start the second request after the first request has been completed, and each request takes around 2-3 seconds.

We can't do anything about the terribly slow remote web service, but our own code isn't exactly optimal either. Our two requests don't inherently depend on each other, and yet, we are executing them serially.

Of course starting these requests in parallel is simple, because both are asynchronous operations:

```
'use strict';

var request = require('request');
```

```
var name, status;

request.get(
  'http://localhost:8080/getUserName?id=1234',
  function(err, res, body) {
    var result = JSON.parse(body);
    name = result.value;
});

request.get(
  'http://localhost:8080/getUserStatus?id=1234',
  function(err, res, body) {
    var result = JSON.parse(body);
    status = result.value;
});

console.log('The status of user', name, 'is', status);
```

No, wait, sorry! That's not going to work – `console.log` will execute within the first event loop iteration while the request callbacks are triggered in later iterations. Mh, how about...

```
'use strict';

var request = require('request');

var name, status;

request.get(
  'http://localhost:8080/getUserName?id=1234',
  function(err, res, body) {
    var result = JSON.parse(body);
    name = result.value;
});

request.get(
  'http://localhost:8080/getUserStatus?id=1234',
  function(err, res, body) {
    var result = JSON.parse(body);
    status = result.value;

    console.log('The status of user', name, 'is', status);
});
```

No, that's not good either: We *start* both request in parallel, but we have no guarantee that they will finish at the same time. We risk printing `The status of user undefined is 75` if the second request finishes earlier than the first. Well, looks like we need some additional code to synchronize our finished calls. How about this:

```
'use strict';

var request = require('request');

var name, status;
var firstHasFinished, secondHasFinished = false;

request.get(
  'http://localhost:8080/getUserName?id=1234',
  function(err, res, body) {
    var result = JSON.parse(body);
    name = result.value;
    markFinished('first');
});

request.get(
  'http://localhost:8080/getUserStatus?id=1234',
  function(err, res, body) {
    var result = JSON.parse(body);
    status = result.value;
    markFinished('second');
});

function markFinished(step) {
  if (step == 'first') {
    firstHasFinished = true;
  }

  if (step == 'second') {
    secondHasFinished = true;
  }

  if (firstHasFinished && secondHasFinished) {
    console.log('The status of user', name, 'is', status);
  }
}
```

Seriously now – that's not even funny! What if we need to synchronize dozens or hundreds of operations? We could use an array where we store the state of each operation... no, this whole thing doesn't feel right.

The `async` module to the rescue, I say!

The `async` moduleis a clever little module that makes managing complex control flows in our code a breeze.

After installing the module via `npm install async@2.1.4`, we can write our client like this:

```
'use strict';

var request = require('request');
var async = require('async');

var name, status;

var getUsername = function(callback) {
  request.get(
    'http://localhost:8080/getUserName?id=1234',
    function(err, res, body) {
      var result = JSON.parse(body);
      callback(err, result.value);
    });
};

var getUserStatus = function(callback) {
  request.get(
    'http://localhost:8080/getUserStatus?id=1234',
    function (err, res, body) {
      var result = JSON.parse(body);
      callback(err, result.value);
    });
};

async.parallel([getUsername, getUserStatus], function(err, results) {
  console.log('The status of user', results[0], 'is', results[1]);
});
```

Let's analyze what we are doing here.

In `var async = require('async');` line, we load the `async` library. We then wrap our requests into named functions. These functions will be called with a `callback` parameter. Inside our functions, we trigger this callback when our operation has finished – in this case, when the requests have been answered.

We call the callbacks with two parameters: an *error* object (which is *null* if no errors occured), and the result value.

The orchestration happens from the `async.parallel([getUsername,` `getUserStatus], function(err, results) {` line until the last line. We use the `parallel` method of the `async` object and pass an array of all the functions we want to run in parallel. Additionally, we pass a `callback` function which expect two parameters, *err* and *results*.

`async.parallel` will trigger this callback as soon as the slowest of the parallel operations has finished (and called its callback), or as soon as one of the operations triggers its callback with an error.

Let's see what this does to the total runtime of our script:

```
$ time node client.js
The status of user 95 is 54
real    0m3.176s
user    0m0.240s
sys     0m0.044s
```

As one would expect, the total runtime of our own code matches the runtime of one request because both requests are started in parallel and will finish roughly at the same time.

Optimizing code structure with async

The `async` module offers several other mechanisms for managing the control flow of our code. These are interesting even if our concern isn't performance optimization. Let's investigate them.

For these cases, let's remove the artificial slowness from the API server by removing the `setTimeout` operation, making the server respond immediately:

```
'use strict';

var http = require('http');
var url = require('url');
var querystring = require('querystring');

http.createServer(function(request, response) {

  var pathname = url.parse(request.url).pathname;
  var query = url.parse(request.url).query;
  var id = querystring.parse(query)['id'];
```

```
    var result = {
      'pathname': pathname,
      'id': id,
      'value': Math.floor(Math.random() * 100)
    };

    response.writeHead(200, {"Content-Type": "application/json"});
    response.end(JSON.stringify(result));

}).listen(
  8080,
  function() {
    console.log('Echo Server listening on port 8080');
  }
);
```

Sometimes we want to run operations in series. This is of course possible by putting method calls into the callback functions of previous method calls, but the code quickly becomes ugly if you do this with a lot of methods:

```
'use strict';

var request = require('request');

var url = 'http://localhost:8080/';

request.get(url + 'getUserName?id=1234', function(err, res, body) {
  console.log('Name:', JSON.parse(body).value);

  request.get(url + 'getUserStatus?id=1234', function(err, res, body) {
    console.log('Status:', JSON.parse(body).value);

    request.get(url + 'getUserCountry?id=1234', function(err, res,
    body) {
      console.log('Country:', JSON.parse(body).value);

      request.get(url + 'getUserAge?id=1234', function(err, res, body)
      {
        console.log('Age:', JSON.parse(body).value);
      });

    });

  });

});
```

This is already starting to look messy, and we haven't even added any notable *business logic* to our code.

Note how our code is intended another level with every method call, creating the so-called *boomerang pattern* that is typical for multi-level nested callback control flows.

We can use `async.series` to achieve the same control flow with much cleaner code:

```
'use strict';

var request = require('request');
var async = require('async');
var url = 'http://localhost:8080/';

async.series([

  function(callback) {
    request.get(url + 'getUserName?id=1234', function(err, res, body) {
      console.log('Name:', JSON.parse(body).value);
      callback(null);
    });
  },

  function(callback) {
    request.get(url + 'getUserStatus?id=1234', function(err, res, body) {
      console.log('Status:', JSON.parse(body).value);
      callback(null);
    });
  },

  function(callback) {
    request.get(url + 'getUserCountry?id=1234', function(err, res,
    body) {
      console.log('Country:', JSON.parse(body).value);
      callback(null);
    });
  },

  function(callback) {
    request.get(url + 'getUserAge?id=1234', function(err, res, body) {
      console.log('Age:', JSON.parse(body).value);
      callback(null);
    });
  }

]);
```

Just as with `async.parallel`, we can use `async.series` to collect the results of each step and do something with them once all steps have finished. This is again achieved by passing the result of each step to the callback each step triggers, and by providing a callback function to the `async.series` call which will receive an array of all results:

```
'use strict';

var request = require('request');
var async = require('async');
var url = 'http://localhost:8080/';

async.series([

  function(callback) {
    request.get(url + 'getUserName?id=1234', function(err, res, body) {
      callback(null, 'Name: ' + JSON.parse(body).value);
    });
  },

  function(callback) {
    request.get(url + 'getUserStatus?id=1234', function(err, res, body) {
      callback(null, 'Status: ' + JSON.parse(body).value);
    });
  },

  function(callback) {
    request.get(url + 'getUserCountry?id=1234', function(err, res,
    body) {
      callback(null, 'Country: ' + JSON.parse(body).value);
    });
  },

  function(callback) {
    request.get(url + 'getUserAge?id=1234', function(err, res, body) {
      callback(null, 'Age: ' + JSON.parse(body).value);
    });
  }

],

  function(err, results) {
    for (var i=0; i < results.length; i++) {
      console.log(results[i]);
    }
  }

);
```

In case that one of the series steps passes a non-null value to its callback as the first parameter, the series is immediately stopped, and the final callback is triggered with the results that have been collected to far, and the `err` parameter set to the error value passed by the failing step.

`async.waterfall` is similar to `async.series`, as it executes all steps in series, but it also enables us to access the results of a previous step in the step that follows:

```
'use strict';

var request = require('request');
var async = require('async');

var url = 'http://localhost:8080/';

async.waterfall([

    function(callback) {
      request.get(url + 'getSessionId', function(err, res, body) {
        callback(null, JSON.parse(body).value);
      });
    },

    function(sId, callback) {
      request.get(url + 'getUserId?sessionId=' + sId, function(err,
      res, body) {
        callback(null, sId, JSON.parse(body).value);
      });
    },

    function(sId, uId, callback) {
      request.get(url + 'getUserName?userId=' + uId, function(err, res,
      body) {
        callback(null, JSON.parse(body).value, sId);
      });
    }

  ],

  function(err, name, sId) {
    console.log('Name:', name);
    console.log('SessionID:', sId);
  }

);
```

Note how for each step function, `callback` is passed as the last argument. It follows a list of arguments for each parameter that is passed by the previous function, minus the error argument which each step function always passes as the first parameter to the `callback` function.

Also note the difference in the final callback: instead of results, it too expects a list of result values, passed by the last waterfall step.

The `async` module provides several other interesting methods which help us to bring order in our control flow and allows us to orchestrate tasks in an efficient manner. Check out *the async documentation*(`http://caolan.github.io/async/`) for more details.

7
Node.js and MySQL

Using the mysql library

Node.js is able to connect to MySQL database servers, but support for this is not built in. We need to make use of a Node.js package that handles the low level details of establishing a connection and talking to the database. Additionally, such a package should enable us to issue statements to the database written in SQL.

The most widely accepted NPM package for this is simply named `mysql`.

In order to use it, let's start by declaring `mysql` as a dependency for our project in our `package.json` file:

```
{
    "dependencies": {
        "mysql": "^2.12.0"
    }
}
```

As always, `npm install` pulls in everything we need to start working with a MySQL database.

For what follows, I assume that you have a working MySQL database up and running on your local machine. You should be able to connect to it locally. You can verify that this is the case by running `mysql -h127.0.0.1 -uroot -p` on your command line. Provide the database root password if needed – you will also need this password in your Node.js code in order to establish a connection.

If you have Docker installed on your machine, the quickest way to get a MySQL server up and running is this one-liner:

```
docker run --rm --name mysql -e MYSQL_ROOT_PASSWORD=my-
secret-pw -p 3306:3306 -d
mysql:5.6
```

See `https://hub.docker.com/_/mysql/` for more details.

A first database application

Once you are up and running, let's start with a first, simple database application. Create a file `index.js` in the directory where you installed the `mysql` module, and fill it with the following code:

```
'use strict';

var mysql = require('mysql');

var connection = mysql.createConnection({
  host: 'localhost',
  user: 'root',
  password: 'root'
});

connection.query(
  'SELECT "foo" AS first_field, "bar" AS second_field',
  function (err, results, fields) {
    console.log(results);
    connection.end();
  }
);
```

Let's see what exactly happens here. First, we include the external `mysql` library at `var mysql = require('mysql'` line. We then create a new object dubbed `connection` in the `var connection = mysql.createConnection({` line.

This object is a representation of our connection with the database. No connection without connecting, which is why we call the `createConnection` function with the parameters necessary to connect and authenticate against the database server: the host name, the username, and the password.

Note that there is a parameter `port` which defaults to `3306` if omitted. You only need to set this parameter if your database server does not run on this default port.

For a list of all possible parameters (a total of 22 are available), see the `mysql` documentation at `https://github.com/mysqljs/mysql#establishing-connections`.

Through the newly created `connection` object, we can now talk to the database server, which is what we do in the `connection.query(` line. To do so, the `connection` object provides a method named `query`.

We provide two parameters to the method call. The first is an SQL statement, the second is an anonymous function. This function gets called when Node.js receives the answer to our query from the server – a *callback*.

This is once again the classical asynchronous pattern of JavaScript applications that makes sense whenever our code triggers an operation whose execution could potentially block the program flow if executed synchronously: Imagine the database needing 5 seconds before it has compiled the answer to our query –that's not unlikely for more complex queries. If we wouldn't wait for the database's answer asynchronously, then our whole application would have to wait for it. No other code could be executed for these 5 seconds, rendering our whole application unusable during this time.

The `'SELECT "foo" AS first_field, "bar" AS second_field'`, line shows which parameters the `query` method passes to our callback function: `err`, `results`, and `fields`.

For now, let's concentrate on `results`, because that's where the fun is.

What kind of thing is `results`? It's simply an array of objects, with each object representing one row of the result set and each attribute of such an object representing one field of the according row.

Let's run our application and examine its output to see how this looks. Please run node `index.js`. The result should look like this:

```
[ RowDataPacket { first_field: 'foo', second_field: 'bar' } ]
```

Let's add a legend:

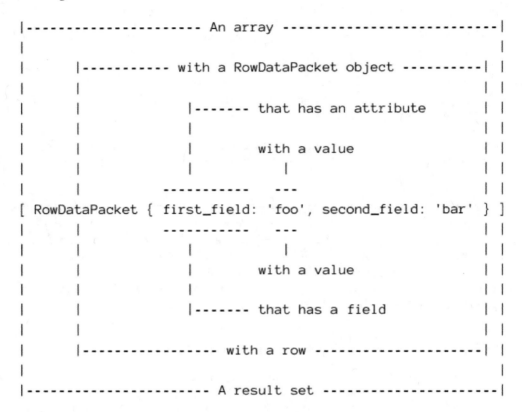

```
|--------------------- An array ---------------------------|
|                                                          |
|          |----------- with a RowDataPacket object ----------| |
|          |                                              | |
|          |                |------- that has an attribute | |
|          |                |                             | |
|          |                |      with a value           | |
|          |                |         |                   | |
|          |         ----------- ---                      | |
[ RowDataPacket { first_field: 'foo', second_field: 'bar' } ]
|          |         ----------- ---                      | |
|          |                |         |                   | |
|          |                |      with a value           | |
|          |                |                             | |
|          |                |------- that has a field     | |
|          |                                              | |
|          |---------------- with a row --------------------| |
|                                                          |
|--------------------- A result set ----------------------|
```

(Note that we didn't query for any real data from any real database table, but relational databases are really stubborn and treat everything as a set of rows of fields, even if we only query for some text strings mapped to made up fields like we just did.)

According to this structure we can of course access the value of any field in any row directly, by accessing the right attribute of the right object:

```
console.log(results[0].first_field); // Outputs 'foo';
```

Let's examine the other parameters that are passed to our anonymous callback function.

err is either an error object, if a problem occured, or *null* if everything went well. Let's modify our code a bit to see how this works:

```
'use strict';

var mysql = require('mysql');

var connection = mysql.createConnection({
  host: 'localhost',
  user: 'root',
  password: 'root'
});

connection.query(
  'SLECT "foo" AS first_field, "bar" AS second_field',
  function (err, results, fields) {
    console.log(err);
    console.log(results);
    connection.end();
  }
);
```

Note how I changed the SQL statement in the 'SLECT "foo" AS first_field, "bar" AS second_field', line and added logging of the err parameter on console.log(err); line. The altered SQL statement is invalid and results in the database answering the query with an error. The mysql library translates this error into an error object which is then passed as the first parameter to our callback function.

If you run the new code, a string representation of the error object is written to the console:

```
{ Error: ER_PARSE_ERROR: You have an error in your SQL syntax; check the
manual that corresponds to your MySQL server version for the right syntax
to use near 'SLECT "foo" AS first_field, "bar" AS second_field' at line 1
...
... a long stacktrace ...
...
code: 'ER_PARSE_ERROR',
errno: 1064,
sqlState: '42000',
index: 0 }
```

The fact that the `err` parameter is *null* if no error occured makes error handling in our code very simple:

```
'use strict';

var mysql = require('mysql');

var connection = mysql.createConnection({
  host: 'localhost',
  user: 'root',
  password: 'root'
});

connection.query(
  'SLECT "foo" AS first_field, "bar" AS second_field',
  function (err, results, fields) {
    if (err) {
      console.log('A database error occured!');
    } else {
      console.log(results);
    }
    connection.end();
  }
);
```

That's a very typical pattern in a lot of Node.js applications: Call a library function while providing a callback, and check if the first parameter passed to this callback is *null* in order to decide if an error occured, continuing otherwise.

`fields` returns an array with one object for every field that was requested in the query – each object contains meta information about the according field. It isn't of any significant use for us here. Feel free to `console.log()` the `fields` parameter if you like.

Using the Streaming API

Next, we will query some real data from existing tables. For this, we first need to create a database, add a table to it, and insert some rows. Let's do this through a Node.js application. Please create a file `create.js` with the following content:

```
'use strict';

var mysql = require('mysql');

var connection = mysql.createConnection({
  host: 'localhost',
```

```
  user: 'root',
  password: 'root'
});

connection.query('CREATE DATABASE node', function(err) {
  if (err) {
    console.log('Could not create database "node".');
  }
});

connection.query('USE node', function(err) {
  if (err) {
    console.log('Could not switch to database "node".');
  }
});

connection.query('CREATE TABLE test ' +
                 '(id INT(11) AUTO_INCREMENT, ' +
                 ' content VARCHAR(255), ' +
                 ' PRIMARY KEY(id))',
  function(err) {
    if (err) {
      console.log('Could not create table "test".');
    }
  }
);

connection.query('INSERT INTO test (content) VALUES ("Hello")');
connection.query('INSERT INTO test (content) VALUES ("World")');

connection.end();
```

This program is meant to be executed just once in order to set up a new database with some example data. Please run it now.

Let's rewrite our index.js file and try to query for this newly added data:

```
'use strict';

var mysql = require('mysql');

var connection = mysql.createConnection({
  host: 'localhost',
  user: 'root',
  password: 'root',
  database: 'node'
});
```

```
connection.query(
  'SELECT id, content FROM test',
  function (err, results, fields) {
    if (err) {
      console.log('A database error occured!');
    } else {
      console.log(results);
    }
    connection.end();
  }
);
```

Please note how on database: 'node' line I have added an additional connection parameter named database. This way, a default database is already selected for subsequent queries on this connection, and doesn't have to be selected through a USE *database* query.

If we execute the script, the result should look like this:

```
[ RowDataPacket { id: 1, content: 'Hello' },
RowDataPacket { id: 2, content: 'World' } ]
```

As one would expect, we now receive an array with two objects, because the result set consists of two rows.

This gives us the opportunity to discuss an even better way to handle result sets from queries.

I have explained how the classical callback pattern should be used on the *query* call because otherwise expensive database operations could block the whole Node.js application.

However, there is another source of potentially blocking behaviour: large result sets.

Imagine that our test database consists of 1,000,000 rows instead of just two, and we would like to output the content of the whole result set to the console like this:

```
connection.query( '
  SELECT id, content FROM test',
  function (err, results, fields) {
    for (var i = 0; i < results.length; i++) {
      console.log('Content of id ' + results[i].id +
                         ' is ' + results[i].content);
    }
  }
);
```

Using the callback pattern ensures that our Node.js application won't block while the database retrieves these 1,000,000 rows. However, once we receive the result set with these rows in our application – that is, within the callback – and we start operating on them, executing these operations also will take a long time.

During this time, our application will block, too. Remember that in Node.js, only one piece of our JavaScript code is executed at any given time. If we iterate over these 1,000,000 array entries and do something with each entry, and this takes, say, 10 seconds, then our application cannot do something else during these 10 seconds.

The solution: instead of using the all-or-nothing callback pattern, we can utilize *mysql's* streaming API.

Instead of providing a callback function to the *query* call, we only provide the SQL statement, but we use the return value of the `query` function: a *Query* object.

This object emits several events that happen during the lifetime of the query: `error`, `field`, `row` and `end`.

Let's concentrate on `row` and see how a more efficient version of our 1,000,000 row output application would look like:

```
var query = connection.query('SELECT id, content FROM test');

query.on('row', function(row) {
  console.log('Content of id ' + row.id + ' is ' + row.content);
});
```

Now we have a piece of our code running 1,000,000 times, once for each row. While this doesn't make our application faster in the narrower sense (it will still take the assumed 10 seconds until all rows have been handled), it does make it way more efficient. Our application now only blocks during the handling of one row, immediately returning control to the event loop of our application, allowing to execute other code in between.

Of course, this isn't critical for an application that is used by only one person on one shell console. But it is *very* critical if such a database operation takes place within a multi-user client-server application:

Imagine you use a website to retrieve a small amount of data from a database – you wouldn't want to wait 10 seconds for your page to load only because another user requested a page that retrieved 1,000,000 rows for him from the database.

Let's rewrite our `index.js` script once again to demonstrate usage of the complete streaming API of the `mysql` library:

```
'use strict';

var mysql = require('mysql');

var connection = mysql.createConnection({
  host: 'localhost',
  user: 'root',
  password: 'root',
  database: 'node'
});

var query = connection.query('SELECT id, content FROM test');

query.on('error', function(err) {
  console.log('A database error occured:');
  console.log(err);
});

query.on('fields', function(fields) {
  console.log('Received fields information.');
});

query.on('result', function(result) {
  console.log('Received result:');
  console.log(result);
});

query.on('end', function() {
  console.log('Query execution has finished.');
  connection.end();
});
```

It's pretty much self explanatory. Note how the order of the on blocks doesn't say anything about when (and if) they are executed – it's up to the `mysql` lib to decide when each block (or, to be more precise: the anonymous callback function associated with each block) will be called.

When executing this script, this is what the output should look like:

```
Received fields information.
Received result:
RowDataPacket { id: 1, content: 'Hello' }
Received result:
RowDataPacket { id: 2, content: 'World' }
Query execution has finished.
```

Making SQL queries secure against attacks

Let's now go full circle and create a simple web application that allows to insert data into our table and also reads and displays the data that was entered.

We need to start a web server with two routes (one for displaying data, one for taking user input), and we need to pass user input to the database and database results to the webpage. Here is the application in one go:

```
'use strict';

var mysql       = require('mysql'),
    http        = require('http'),
    url         = require('url'),
    querystring = require('querystring');


// Start a web server on port 8888. Requests go to function handleRequest

http.createServer(handleRequest).listen(8888);


// Function that handles http requests

function handleRequest(request, response) {

  // Page HTML as one big string, with placeholder "DBCONTENT" for data
  // from the database
  var pageContent = '<html>' +
                    '<head>' +
                    '<meta http-equiv="Content-Type" ' +
                    'content="text/html; charset=UTF-8" />' +
                    '</head>' +
                    '<body>' +
                    '<form action="/add" method="post">' +
                    '<input type="text" name="content">' +
                    '<input type="submit" value="Add content" />' +
```

```
                    '</form>' +
                    '<div>' +
                    '<strong>Content in database:</strong>' +
                    '<pre>' +
                    'DBCONTENT' +
                    '</pre>' +
                    '</div>' +
                    '<form action="/" method="get">' +
                    '<input type="text" name="q">' +
                    '<input type="submit" value="Filter content" />' +
                    '</form>' +
                    '</body>' +
                    '</html>';

    // Parsing the requested URL path in order to distinguish between
    // the / page and the /add route
    var pathname = url.parse(request.url).pathname;

    // User wants to add content to the database (POST request to /add)
    if (pathname == '/add') {
      var requestBody = '';
      var postParameters;
      request.on('data', function (data) {
        requestBody += data;
      });
      request.on('end', function() {
        postParameters = querystring.parse(requestBody);
        // The content to be added is in POST parameter "content"
        addContentToDatabase(postParameters.content, function() {
          // Redirect back to homepage when the database has finished
          // adding the new content to the database
          response.writeHead(302, {'Location': '/'});
          response.end();
        });
      });

    // User wants to read data from the database (GET request to /)
    } else {
      // The text to use for filtering is in GET parameter "q"
      var filter = querystring.parse(url.parse(request.url).query).q;
      getContentsFromDatabase(filter, function(contents) {
        response.writeHead(200, {'Content-Type': 'text/html'});
        // Poor man's templating system: Replace "DBCONTENT" in page HTML
        // with the actual content we received from the database
        response.write(pageContent.replace('DBCONTENT', contents));
        response.end();
      });
    }
```

```
}


// Function that is called by the code that handles the / route and
// retrieves contents from the database, applying a LIKE filter if one
// was supplied

function getContentsFromDatabase(filter, callback) {
  var connection = mysql.createConnection({
    host: 'localhost',
    user: 'root',
    password: 'root',
    database: 'node'
  });
  var query;
  var resultsAsString = '';

  if (filter) {
    query = connection.query('SELECT id, content FROM test ' +
                             'WHERE content LIKE "' + filter + '%"');
  } else {
    query = connection.query('SELECT id, content FROM test');
  }

  query.on('error', function(err) {
    console.log('A database error occured:');
    console.log(err);
  });

  // With every result, build the string that is later replaced into
  // the HTML of the homepage
  query.on('result', function(result) {
    resultsAsString += 'id: ' + result.id;
    resultsAsString += ', content: ' + result.content;
    resultsAsString += 'n';
  });

  // When we have worked through all results, we call the callback
  // with our completed string
  query.on('end', function(result) {
    connection.end();
    callback(resultsAsString);
  });
}


// Function that is called by the code that handles the /add route
// and inserts the supplied string as a new content entry
```

```
function addContentToDatabase(content, callback) {
  var connection = mysql.createConnection({
    host: 'localhost',
    user: 'root',
    password: 'root',
    database: 'node'
  });

  connection.query('INSERT INTO test (content) ' +
                   'VALUES ("' + content + '")',
    function(err) {
      if (err) {
        console.log('Could not insert content "' + content +
                   '" into database.');
      }
      callback();
    });
}
```

Simply start the application by running `node index.js`, open up its homepage in your browser by visiting `http://localhost:8888/`, and play around with it.

So, that's quite a bit of code here. Let's walk through the important parts. If the user requests the homepage, here is what happens:

- The HTTP server that is started in the `http.createServer(handleRequest).listen(8888);` line receives the requests and calls the `handleRequest` function that is declared in the `function handleRequest(request, response) {` line.
- In the `var pathname = url.parse(request.url).pathname;` line the variable `pathname` is declared and initialized with the requested path, which is / in this case, by parsing the request URL.
- The code continues in the `} else {` line, where the request for / is handled.
- The handling starts by parsing the URL for the value of the GET parameter `q` which is later used to filter the database content.
- In the `getContentsFromDatabase(filter, function(contents) {` line things start to get interesting. We call `getContentsFromDatabase` with two parameters: The `filter` string we just parsed from the URL, and an anonymous callback function.

- Execution continues in `function getContentsFromDatabase(filter, callback) {` line, starting with the creation of a new database connection.
- Then, from `if (filter) {` line to `query = connection.query( 'SELECT id, content FROM test' );}` line, the query to retrieve the contents from the database is started.
- Each retrieved row triggers the execution of the `result` event handler in the `query.on( 'result' , function(result) {` line, where we extend the string `resultsAsString` with the contents of each row.
- Execution jumps to `query.on( 'end' , function(result) {` line once all rows have been retrieved. Here, in the `end` event handler, we close the connection to the database and then call the callback we passed into the `getContentsFromDatabase` function. This returns control back to the request handler, in `response.writeHead( 200, { 'Content-Type' : 'text/html' });` line.
- There, we start responding to the request, first by sending a status 200 header, followed by the page content – with the database content replaced into the HTML at the proper place in the `response.end();` line.

With this, the request has been handled and responded to.

When the user uses the `Filter content` form, the same procedure is executed, with the only difference that now the GET parameter `q` has a value which is then used to filter the database results using the SQL `LIKE` clause.

When using the `Add content` button, a different execution path is taken:

- The HTTP server that is started in the `http.createServer(handleRequest).listen( 8888);` line receives the requests and calls the `handleRequest` function that is declared in the `function handleRequest(request, response) {` line.
- In the `var pathname = url.parse(request.url).pathname;` line the variable `pathname` is declared and initialized with the requested path, which is `/add` in this case, by parsing the request URL.
- The code continues in the `if (pathname == '/add' ) {` line, where the request for `/add` is handled.

- Then, on `request.on( 'data' , function (data) {` line, the body of the request (the POST data) is retrieved step-by-step, in the same way that large result sets from a database can be retrieved when using the streaming API. With every step, a variable is extended which finally holds the complete request body.
- Once the request has been fully received, execution continues in the `request.on( 'end' , function() {` line when the `end` event is triggered for the request.
- We then parse the request body in order to translate the POST data into a JavaScript object which allows us to easily access the value of POST parameters, as is done in the `addContentToDatabase(postParameters.content,` `function() {` line where we call the `addContentToDatabase` function with the string that is to be added to the database as its first parameter, followed by a callback function that we expect to be triggered once the data has been inserted.
- With this, execution continues in the `function` `addContentToDatabase(content, callback) {` line where we start by connecting to the database, followed by an `INSERT` query in the `connection.query( 'INSERT INTO test (content) ' +` line. The `query` function triggers our anonymous callback defined on `'VALUES ("' +` `content + '")'` , line when the query execution has finished, which in turn triggers the callback that was passed in from the request handler function.
- This leads to execution continuing in the `response.writeHead( 302, {` `'Location' : '/' });` line, where we redirect the user's browser back to the homepage.

So, nice application, does what it's supposed to do. And has a huge problem.

Why? Because the way we treat the incoming data that is provided by the user puts our database at risk. Our application is vulnerable to so-called SQL injection attacks. Let's demonstrate how.

To do so, let's create another table within our database `node`, one that's supposed to carry sensitive information that's not meant for any user's eyes. We will just pretend that our nice little content-viewer app is part of a bigger application that somewhere also stores user passwords.

We will call this table `passwords`, and you need to create this within the `node` database on your local server, either using the MySQL command line, a MySQL GUI client you happen to use, or, if you like, you can simply rewrite the `create.js` script we used earlier, like this:

```
'use strict';

var mysql = require('mysql');

var connection = mysql.createConnection({
  host: 'localhost',
  user: 'root',
  password: 'root'
});

connection.query('USE node', function(err) {
  if (err) {
    console.log('Could not switch to database "node".');
  }
});

connection.query('CREATE TABLE passwords ' +
                 '(id INT(11) AUTO_INCREMENT, ' +
                 ' password VARCHAR(255), ' +
                 ' PRIMARY KEY(id))',
  function(err) {
    if (err) {
      console.log('Could not create table "passwords".');
    }
  }
);

connection.query('INSERT INTO passwords (password) VALUES ("secret")');
connection.query('INSERT INTO passwords (password) VALUES ("dont_tell")');

connection.end();
```

Execute `create.js` through Node.js in order to create the new table.

Now, here is the scenario: We have a table `test` that contains public information, and a table `passwords` that contains sensitive information. We have written an application that operates only on the `test` table, thus allowing public access to the public information in that table, but not allowing access to any sensitive information like the passwords in the `passwords` table.

And yet, the passwords can be retrieved through the application. Here's how to do that:

- Start the application with `node index.js`
- Visit `http://localhost:8888` in your browser
- Enter the following text into the second text input field and hit **Filter content**

```
%" UNION SELECT id, password AS content FROM passwords WHERE
password LIKE "
```

Note that you need to enter the text *exactly* as shown above, starting with a percentage sign and ending with a quotation mark.

You will receive a list of data from the `test` table (if any content has been added before), but at the end of this list, you will also see the two passwords we have added to the `passwords` table, like this:

```
id: 1, content: foo bar
id: 1, content: secret
id: 2, content: dont_tell
```

Whoops. How is that possible? It's because a set of SQL commands has been injected into our application's SQL, although only data – the string to filter for – was meant to be injected. Hence an SQL injection attack.

If you look at the critical piece of our code, what happens becomes clear. In the

```
query = connection.query('SELECT id, content FROM test ' + 'WHERE
content LIKE "' + filter + '%"');
```
line, our SQL query is constructed:

If the content of the `filter` variable is `foo`, this is what the final SQL looks like:

```
SELECT id, content FROM test WHERE content LIKE "foo%"
```

But if the malicious filter text is entered into the web page, we end up with the following SQL query:

```
SELECT id, content FROM test WHERE content LIKE "%" UNION
    SELECT id, password AS content FROM passwords WHERE password LIKE "%"
```

(I've added a line break in order to stay within the boundaries of the text page.)

The malicious filter text simply closes the LIKE query of the original SQL and continues with an additional SELECT on the passwords table, combining the results of both SELECTs into a single (and identically structured) result set using the UNION clause. Another LIKE clause is added at the end of the malicious code, which makes sure that the whole SQL is syntactically correct.

This is a made up example for demo purposes, but that's how actual attacks look like. A real attack might need a lot more effort – for example, the attacker needs to find out the structure of the passwords table, but supporting information can be gathered by querying meta data from the database; if an attacker finds a part of the application that allows to extend harmless SQL queries into more potent ones, finding sensitive information is only a question of time and patience.

What can we, as application developers, do against such attacks? There is no 100% secure system, as the saying goes, however, there are a lot of ways to raise the bar, making attacks more difficult.

In our scenario, a very effective counter-measure is to use placeholders with value assignment when building SQL statements, instead of hand-crafting the final query by concatenating strings.

This way, we can guarantee that any part of your query that is supposed to be treated as a value is indeed interpreted by the mysql library as a value, escaping it in a way that doesn't allow the value to end up at the database server as a command.

To achieve this, we need a way to create a query that can unambiguously differentiate between the command parts of a query and the value parts.

This is done by creating a query where the value parts are not directly included within the query string –instead, their position is marked with a special character, the quotation mark ?, as a placeholder.

This is how our query looks when using this syntax:

```
SELECT id, content FROM test WHERE content LIKE ?
```

Now the mysql library knows that whatever is going to be used at the position marked by the ? placeholder is a value, treating it accordingly.

Of course, when issuing the query, we also need a way to tell what value to use. This is done by mapping the value onto the query-with-placeholder, like so:

```
filter = filter + '%';
query = connection.query('SELECT id, content FROM test WHERE content LIKE
?', filter);
```

In our specific case, we need to add the search wildcard, %, to the filter parameter. We then construct the query with the placeholder, passing the value for this placeholder as the second parameter. The rest of the code remains unchanged.

We should change the INSERT query that is used for adding content, too, by rewriting the code:

```
connection.query('INSERT INTO test (content) ' + 'VALUES ("' + content
+ '")',
```

The changed line is as follows:

```
connection.query('INSERT INTO test (content) VALUES (?)', content,
  function(err) {
  . . .
```

This changes the SQL query to placeholder syntax, and adds the content variable as the second parameter. The callback function is now the third parameter.

Mapping multiple values onto multiple placeholders is done by providing an array of values:

```
query('SELECT foo FROM bar WHERE id = ? AND name = ?', [42, 'John Doe']);
```

Here, 42 maps to the id placeholder, and John Doe to the name placeholder.

If you restart the application ad try to attack it again, you will see that the attack no longer works. Mission accomplished.

Summary

In this chapter we learned about the mysql module, how it enables us to connect to relational databases, how using asynchronous callbacks and the Streaming API enable us to write efficient applications even when large result sets need to be handled, and analyzed how database applications can be attacked and, more importantly, how we can protect our applications against these kinds of attacks.

8
Node.js and MongoDB

Some MongoDB basics

MongoDB is a document-oriented NoSQL database that stores objects in the following hierarchy:

```
Server
    \_Database
            \_Collection
                        \_Document
                        \_Document
                        \_Document
                        \_ ...
            \_Collection
                        \_Document
                        \_Document
                        \_Document
                        \_ ...
```

If you are coming from a relational SQL database background (I do), then it might help to think of collections as tables, and of documents as rows in that table. It's not a perfect analogy, however; the key idea of a document-oriented database like MongoDB is that documents within the same collection do not need to have the same structure, while each row in a table of a relational database does have the same structure.

Here is how actual data in this hierarchy might actually look like:

```
localhost
    \_accounting
        \_customers
            \_ { _id: 53c6c2, name: 'Jane Doe' }
            \_ { _id: 9dc42e, name: 'John Doe', age: 24 }
            \_ { _id: 63a76d, name: 'Jim Doe', options: { billtime: 3 } }
        \_invoices
            \_ { _id: 98ef5a, value: 192.87 }
            \_ { _id: f4eb21, value: 192.87, recurring: true }
```

This example represents the case where one has a MongoDB server running on localhost, with two databases `customers` and `invoices`. Each database contains some documents that are similar, but not identical, in structure.

As you can see, I have represented the document objects in JavaScript object notation – this is how we are going to encounter them when working with a MongoDB server from within Node.js.

Every document has an `_id` attribute, which is a random 24-digit hex value – I have shortened them for the illustration.

We will now examine how to create and work with such a structure.

Applying CRUD operations with the low-level mongodb driver

Again, I won't cover installation of the server software. Please refer to *the official installation instructions*(https://docs.mongodb.com/manual/installation/) in order to get a MongoDB server up and running on your machine.

If you have Docker installed on your machine, the quickest way to get a MongoDB server up and running is this one-liner:

```
docker run --rm --name mongo -p 27017:27017 -d mongo:3.4
```

See `https://hub.docker.com/_/mongo/` for more details.

Once this is done, create a new project folder called `mongodb-test`, and in there create an initial `package.json` as follows:

```json
{
    "name": "mongodb-test",
    "version": "0.0.1",
    "description": "",
    "dependencies": {
      "mongodb": "^2.2.22"
    },
    "devDependencies": {}
}
```

As always, we pull in the dependencies with

`npm install`

Now we can create a first program in file `index.js`:

```js
'use strict';

var MongoClient = require('mongodb').MongoClient;

MongoClient.connect(
    'mongodb://127.0.0.1:27017/accounting',
    function(err, connection) {
      var collection = connection.collection('customers');

      collection.insert({'name': 'Jane Doe'}, function(err, count) {

        collection.find().toArray(function(err, documents) {
          console.dir(documents);
          connection.close();
        });

      });

    });
```

Let's see what this code does. In the `var MongoClient = require( 'mongodb' ).MongoClient;` line, we require the `MongoClient` class from the `mongodb` library. We use the `connect` method of this class in the `MongoClient.connect(` line to establish a connection to our MongoDB server, which is listening on `localhost`, port `27017`. Upon connecting, we declare that we want to use the `accounting` database.

We then create an object `collection` in the `var collection = connection.collection( 'customers' );` line which represents the `customers` collection within the `accounting` database.

Using the `insert` method of the `collection` object, we add a new document to the customers collection in the `collection.insert({ 'name' : 'Jane Doe' },` `function(err, count) {` line.

When the insert operation has finished, we query the collection for all existing documents using the `find` method in the `collection.find().toArray( function(err,` `documents) {` line. Our callback receives an array with the documents, prints them to the screen, and then closes the database connection.

Running this code by executing `node index.js` will result in output similar to `[ { _id: 53c8ba1b517c86d3c9df71e6, name: 'Jane Doe' } ]` and running it again will result in output similar to:

```
[ { id: 53c8ba1b517c86d3c9df71e6, name: 'Jane Doe' },
  { id: 53c8ba21d13eb8dbc96e2c19, name: 'Jane Doe' } ]
```

As you can see, each run creates a new document in the database. The `name` attribute is set by our code, the `_id` is generated by MongoDB.

Let's rewrite our code a bit in order to update existing documents:

```
'use strict';

var MongoClient = require('mongodb').MongoClient;

MongoClient.connect(
  'mongodb://127.0.0.1:27017/accounting',
  function(err, connection) {
    var collection = connection.collection('customers');

    collection.update({}, {'$set': {'age': 24}}, function(err, count) {

      console.log('Updated', count, 'documents');

      collection.find().toArray(function(err, documents) {
```

```
            console.dir(documents);
            connection.close();
        });

    });

});
```

The change is in the `collection.update({}, { '$set' : { 'age' : 24}}`, `function(err, count) {` line. Instead of inserting a new document, we want to update our documents. The first parameter is the filter that defines which documents to match when applying the update. In this case, we pass an empty object, that is, we don't want to match any specific document and instead we want to apply the update to all documents in the collection.

The second parameter defines what to update within each matched document. In this case, we want to set the `age` attribute of the documents to *24*. The documents we already stored do not have an `age` attribute yet, but that's not a problem: because MongoDB works schema-less, it will happily add attributes that did not yet exist on a given document.

This is how the content of our collection looks like after running the new code:

```
Updated 1 documents
[ { _id: 53c8ba1b517c86d3c9df71e6, name: 'Jane Doe' },
  { _id: 53c8ba21d13eb8dbc96e2c19, name: 'Jane Doe', age: 24 } ]
```

Oh, well. Not quite what we expected – we didn't define a filter to the `update` statement because we wanted to match all existing documents, and yet only one of our two documents has been updated with the `age` attribute.

The reason is that this is the default behaviour for MongoDB updates: only the first match for a given filter - even if it matches every document - is updated.

Changing the following line:

```
collection.update({}, {'$set': {'age': 24}}, function(err, count) {
```

The changed line is as follows:

```
collection.update(
  {},
  {'$set': {'age': 24}},
  {'multi': true},
  function(err, count) {
```

(that is, by adding a parameter {'multi': true}), we override this behaviour, which then results in MongoDB updating all matching documents.

Let's have a look at how actual filters that match only some of our documents look like. We are going to rewrite our script because we need some more documents to play with:

```
'use strict';

var MongoClient = require('mongodb').MongoClient;

MongoClient.connect(
  'mongodb://127.0.0.1:27017/accounting',
  function (err, connection) {
    var collection = connection.collection('customers');

    var doFind = function (callback) {
      collection.find().toArray(function (err, documents) {
        console.dir(documents);
        callback();
      });
    };

    var doInsert = function (i) {
      if (i < 20) {
        var value = Math.floor(Math.random() * 10);
        collection.insert(
          {'n': '#' + i, 'v': value},
          function (err, count) {
            doInsert(i + 1);
          });
      } else {
        console.log();
        console.log('Inserted', i, 'documents:');
        doFind(function () {
          doUpdate();
        });
      }
    };

    var doUpdate = function () {
      collection.update(
        {'v': {'$gt': 5}},
        {'$set': {'valuable': true}},
        {'multi': true},
        function (err, count) {
          console.log();
          console.log('Updated', count, 'documents:');
          doFind(function () {
```

```
            collection.remove({}, function () {
                connection.close();
            });
        });
    });
};

doInsert(0);

});
```

As you can see, we created three functions, doFind, doInsert and doUpdate. The script starts by calling doInsert, which is a recursive function that inserts 20 documents into the collection, and does so in a serial fashion by recursively calling itself (in the doInsert(i + 1); line) every time the previous insert operation has finished. Each documents has an n attribute with the serial number of its insert operation, and a v value, which is a random number between 0 and 9.

As soon as the limit of 20 inserts has been reached, the function calls doFind (in the doFind(function () { line) which prints all existing documents to the screen. We pass doFind a callback function which calls doUpdate. This function adds the field valuable to some, but not all, documents.

Whether a document is updated or not depends on it's v value: using the $gt operator (in the { 'v' : { '$gt' : 5}}, line), we filter the documents that are affected by the update to those whose value is *greater than* 5.

After the update operation has finished, doFind is called once again, printing the results of the update to the screen. We then delete all documents using remove (in the collection.remove({}, function () { line), again using a filter that matches any document – however, *remove* doesn't need a multi parameter in order to work on all matched documents; it does so by default.

Here is a typical result for a run of this script:

```
Inserted 20 documents:
[ { id: 53d60cc676371927029f95bd, n: '#0', v: 5 },
  { id: 53d60cc676371927029f95be, n: '#1', v: 8 },
  { id: 53d60cc676371927029f95bf, n: '#2', v: 0 },
  { id: 53d60cc676371927029f95c0, n: '#3', v: 4 },
  { id: 53d60cc676371927029f95c1, n: '#4', v: 6 },
  { id: 53d60cc676371927029f95c2, n: '#5', v: 2 },
  { id: 53d60cc676371927029f95c3, n: '#6', v: 4 },
  { id: 53d60cc676371927029f95c4, n: '#7', v: 1 },
  { id: 53d60cc676371927029f95c5, n: '#8', v: 0 },
```

```
{ id: 53d60cc676371927029f95c6, n: '#9',  v: 7 },
{ id: 53d60cc676371927029f95c7, n: '#10', v: 5 },
{ id: 53d60cc676371927029f95c8, n: '#11', v: 8 },
{ id: 53d60cc676371927029f95c9, n: '#12', v: 2 },
{ id: 53d60cc676371927029f95ca, n: '#13', v: 8 },
{ id: 53d60cc676371927029f95cb, n: '#14', v: 1 },
{ id: 53d60cc676371927029f95cc, n: '#15', v: 0 },
{ id: 53d60cc676371927029f95cd, n: '#16', v: 1 },
{ id: 53d60cc676371927029f95ce, n: '#17', v: 4 },
{ id: 53d60cc676371927029f95cf, n: '#18', v: 4 },
{ id: 53d60cc676371927029f95d0, n: '#19', v: 6 } ]

Updated 6 documents:
[ { _id: 53d60cc676371927029f95bd, n: '#0',  v: 5 },
  { _id: 53d60cc676371927029f95bf, n: '#2',  v: 0 },
  { _id: 53d60cc676371927029f95c0, n: '#3',  v: 4 },
  { _id: 53d60cc676371927029f95c2, n: '#5',  v: 2 },
  { _id: 53d60cc676371927029f95c3, n: '#6',  v: 4 },
  { _id: 53d60cc676371927029f95c4, n: '#7',  v: 1 },
  { _id: 53d60cc676371927029f95c5, n: '#8',  v: 0 },
  { _id: 53d60cc676371927029f95c7, n: '#10', v: 5 },
  { _id: 53d60cc676371927029f95c9, n: '#12', v: 2 },
  { _id: 53d60cc676371927029f95cb, n: '#14', v: 1 },
  { _id: 53d60cc676371927029f95cc, n: '#15', v: 0 },
  { _id: 53d60cc676371927029f95cd, n: '#16', v: 1 },
  { _id: 53d60cc676371927029f95ce, n: '#17', v: 4 },
  { _id: 53d60cc676371927029f95cf, n: '#18', v: 4 },
  { _id: 53d60cc676371927029f95be, n: '#1',  v: 8,
    valuable: true },
  { _id: 53d60cc676371927029f95c1, n: '#4',  v: 6,
    valuable: true },
  { _id: 53d60cc676371927029f95c6, n: '#9',  v: 7,
    valuable: true },
  { _id: 53d60cc676371927029f95c8, n: '#11', v: 8,
    valuable: true },
  { _id: 53d60cc676371927029f95ca, n: '#13', v: 8,
    valuable: true },
  { _id: 53d60cc676371927029f95d0, n: '#19', v: 6,
    valuable: true } ]
```

As you can see, 20 documents with a random v value are inserted. Afterwards, all documents whose value is greater than 5 have been updated to include the attribute `valuable` set to `true` – a total of 6 documents in this case.

Retrieving specific documents using filters

We have not yet performed any truly interesting queries against our collection. Up until now, all we did was to retrieve all documents contained in our collection by performing `collection.find()` without any filter. More complex filters are available of course.

Let's rewrite the existing code in order to retrieve only specific documents in our `doFind` function. First, a very simple example – we are going to retrieve all documents where the `v` attribute has a value of 5. Let's change the following line:

```
collection.find().toArray(function (err, documents) {
```

The preceding line is changed to:

```
collection.find({'v': 5}).toArray(function (err, documents) {
```

The preceding changes result in only the matching documents being printed:

```
Inserted 20 documents:
[ { id: 53d7698d99c6107303ad204c, n: '#8', v: 5 },
{ id: 53d7698d99c6107303ad2050, n: '#12', v: 5 } ]

Updated 10 documents:
[ { _id: 53d7698d99c6107303ad204c, n: '#8', v: 5 },
  { _id: 53d7698d99c6107303ad2050, n: '#12', v: 5 } ]
```

We can write filters that match more than just one attribute, like this:

```
collection.find(
  {
    'v': 6,
    'valuable': true
  }
).toArray(function (err, documents) {
```

Both attributes of each document in the collection must match the given values for a document to be included. In other words, this is an AND query.

For the given collection, the preceding query doesn't make too much sense, because after the update, every document with a v value of 6 has the `valuable` attribute set to `true` anyways. But we might want to filter for all `valuable` documents whose v value is less than 8, like so:

```
collection.find(
  {
    'v': { '$lt': 8 },
    'valuable': true
  }
).toArray(function (err, documents) {
```

We already encountered the *greater than* operator `$gt` , and `$lt` is the opposite operator, *less than*. Other available operators are:

- `$lte`: less than or equal
- `$gte`: greater than or equal
- `$ne`: not equal

Filters can also be combined into an OR query, if, for example, we want to query for all documents whose v value is either 5 or 8:

```
collection.find(
  {
    '$or': [
      {'v': 5},
      {'v': 8}
    ]
  }
).toArray(function (err, documents) {
```

And of course it is also possible to combine an AND query and an OR query:

```
collection.find(
  {
    'v': {'$gt': 3},
    '$or': [
      {'n': '#5'},
      {'n': '#10'}
    ]
  }
).toArray(function (err, documents) {
```

This will retrieve all documents that have a v value greater than 3 AND whose n value is #5 OR #10.

Speaking of the n attribute: it holds a string value, which cannot be queried with operators like $gt or $lt, of course. We can, however, apply regular expressions:

```
collection.find(
  {
    'n': /^#1/
  }
).toArray(function (err, documents) {
```

This matches all documents whose n value starts with #1.

All the filter variations discussed so far can also be applied to the update and remove methods of the collection object. This way, you can update or remove only specific documents in a given collection.

The find method also takes an options parameter. Possible options are limit, skip, and sort:

```
collection.find(
  {
    'n': /^#1/
  },
  {
    'limit': 5,
    'skip' : 2,
    'sort' : 'v'
  }
).toArray(function (err, documents) {
```

This one retrieves five documents whose n value starts with #1, skips the first two matches, and sorts the result set by the v value:

```
Inserted 20 documents:
[ { id: 53d7739bbe04f81c05c13b6f, n: '#19', v: 5 }, { id:
53d7739bbe04f81c05c13b66, n: '#10', v: 5 }, { id: 53d7739bbe04f81c05c13b6b,
n: '#15', v: 6 }, { id: 53d7739bbe04f81c05c13b67, n: '#11', v: 7 }, { _id:
53d7739bbe04f81c05c13b68, n: '#12', v: 7 } ]

Updated 9 documents:
[ { _id: 53d7739bbe04f81c05c13b6f, n: '#19', v: 5 },
  { _id: 53d7739bbe04f81c05c13b66, n: '#10', v: 5 },
  { _id: 53d7739bbe04f81c05c13b6b, n: '#15', v: 6,
    valuable: true },
  { _id: 53d7739bbe04f81c05c13b68, n: '#12', v: 7,
    valuable: true },
  { _id: 53d7739bbe04f81c05c13b67, n: '#11', v: 7,
    valuable: true } ]
```

We can also sort over multiple fields and in different directions:

```
collection.find(
  {
    'n': /^#1/
  },
  {
    'limit': 5,
    'skip' : 2,
    'sort' : [ ['v', 'asc'], ['n', 'desc'] ]
  }).toArray(function (err, documents) {
```

This sorts the matching documents first by their v value in ascending order, and documents with an identical v value are then ordered by their n value, in descending order, as can be seen here with the documents whose v value is 1:

```
Inserted 20 documents:
[ { id: 53d77475c0a6e83b0556d817, n: '#14', v: 1 },
  { id: 53d77475c0a6e83b0556d815, n: '#12', v: 1 },
  { id: 53d77475c0a6e83b0556d818, n: '#15', v: 3 },
  { id: 53d77475c0a6e83b0556d81a, n: '#17', v: 4 },
  { _id: 53d77475c0a6e83b0556d814, n: '#11', v: 6 } ]

Updated 7 documents:
[ { _id: 53d77475c0a6e83b0556d817, n: '#14', v: 1 },
  { _id: 53d77475c0a6e83b0556d815, n: '#12', v: 1 },
  { _id: 53d77475c0a6e83b0556d818, n: '#15', v: 3 },
  { _id: 53d77475c0a6e83b0556d81a, n: '#17', v: 4 },
  { _id: 53d77475c0a6e83b0556d814, n: '#11', v: 6, valuable: true } ]
```

More complex update operations

We already learned how to add attributes or change the value of attributes in existing documents:

```
collection.update(
  {'n': /^#1/},
  {'$set': {'v': 5} },
  {'multi': true},
  function (err, count) {
    // ...
  }
```

This would set the value of the v attribute to 5 for all documents whose n value starts with #1.

This is probably the most regularly used update operation. Some other ways to update documents are available, however. Numeric attributes can be increased, for example:

```
collection.update(
  {'n': /^#1/},
  {'$inc': {'v': +1} },
  {'multi': true},
  function (err, count) {
    // ...
  }
```

There is no $dec operation, but of course, we can increase by −1:

```
collection.update(
  {'n': /^#1/},
  {'$inc': {'v': −1} },
  {'multi': true},
  function (err, count) {
    // ...
  }
```

Multiplication is possible, too:

```
collection.update(
  {'n': /^#1/},
  {'$mul': {'v': 2} },
  {'multi': true},
  function (err, count) {
    // ...
  }
```

There are several other operators:

- $rename: Renames a field.
- $unset: Removes the specified field from a document.
- $min: Only updates the field if the specified value is less than the existing field value.
- $max: Only updates the field if the specified value is greater than the existing field value.
- $currentDate Sets the value of a field to current date, either as a Date or a Timestamp.

Please refer to *the MongoDB documentation*(https://docs.mongodb.com/manual/reference/operator/update-field/) for a detailed discussion of each operation.

The update method can be used to perform an operation where documents are updated if the filter being used is able to match existing documents, but a new document is inserted instead if no existing document could be matched. This is called an upsert:

```
collection.update(
  {'n': '#20'},
  {'$set': {'n': '20', 'v': 1} },
  {'multi': true, 'upsert': true},
  function (err, count) {
    // ...
  }
```

In our initial collection, only entries with n from #0 to #19 exist. Therefore, an update call with a filter set to {'n': '#20'} cannot match any document in the collection. Because the upsert option is set to true, a new document is inserted:

```
Inserted 20 documents:
[ { id: 53d789d4fff187d607f03b3a, n: '#0', v: 7 },
  ...
  { id: 53d789d4fff187d607f03b4c, n: '#18', v: 8 },
  { _id: 53d789d4fff187d607f03b4d, n: '#19', v: 5 } ]

Updated 1 documents:
[ { _id: 53d789d4fff187d607f03b3a, n: '#0', v: 7 },
  ...
  { _id: 53d789d4fff187d607f03b4c, n: '#18', v: 8 },
  { _id: 53d789d4fff187d607f03b4d, n: '#19', v: 5 },
  { _id: 53d789d44266a0f5acef6f05, n: '#20', v: 1 } ]
```

Working with indexes

Like other databases, MongoDB needs to index data sets if we want queries on large sets to perform well.

In order to experience this firsthand, let's write a script which inserts 200,000 documents instead of just 20:

```
'use strict';

var MongoClient = require('mongodb').MongoClient;

MongoClient.connect(
  'mongodb://127.0.0.1:27017/accounting',
  function (err, connection) {
    var collection = connection.collection('customers');
```

```
    var doInsert = function (i) {
      if (i < 200000) {
        var value = Math.floor(Math.random() * 10);
        collection.insert(
          {'n': '#' + i, 'v': value},
          function (err, count) {
            doInsert(i + 1);
          });
      } else {
        connection.close();
      }
    };

    doInsert(0);

  });
```

Call this script insert.js and execute it running node insert.js.

Now, we time how long it takes MongoDB to return 10 specific rows from this collection, using the following script:

```
'use strict';

var MongoClient = require('mongodb').MongoClient;

MongoClient.connect(
  'mongodb://127.0.0.1:27017/accounting',
  function (err, connection) {
    var collection = connection.collection('customers');

    collection.find(
      {'v': {'$gt': 5}},
      {
        'skip:': 100000,
        'limit': 10,
        'sort': 'v'
      }
    ).toArray(function (err, documents) {
      console.dir(documents);
        connection.close();
    });

  });
```

This script queries the database for 10 documents whose v attribute is greater than 5, starting at document 100,000, sorting results by their v value.

Name this script `query.js` and run it like this:

```
time node query.js
```

This way, you'll get a poor man's performance benchmark. This is the result on my machine:

```
~$ time node query.js

[ { _id: 53d7955c3ac66b9e0af26745, n: '#36271', v: 6 },
  { _id: 53d7955c3ac66b9e0af26757, n: '#36289', v: 6 },
  { _id: 53d7955c3ac66b9e0af26761, n: '#36299', v: 6 },
  { _id: 53d7955c3ac66b9e0af2677a, n: '#36324', v: 6 },
  { _id: 53d7955c3ac66b9e0af2677b, n: '#36325', v: 6 },
  { _id: 53d7955c3ac66b9e0af26792, n: '#36348', v: 6 },
  { _id: 53d7955c3ac66b9e0af26794, n: '#36350', v: 6 },
  { _id: 53d7955c3ac66b9e0af267b2, n: '#36380', v: 6 },
  { _id: 53d7955c3ac66b9e0af267b3, n: '#36381', v: 6 },
  { _id: 53d7955c3ac66b9e0af267b6, n: '#36384', v: 6 } ]

real  0m1.078s
user  0m0.238s
sys   0m0.040s
```

The script runtime is 1 second on average. Now, write the script that adds an index on the v attribute:

```
'use strict';

var MongoClient = require('mongodb').MongoClient;

MongoClient.connect(
  'mongodb://127.0.0.1:27017/accounting',
  function (err, connection) {
    var collection = connection.collection('customers');

    collection.ensureIndex('v', function(err, indexName) {
      connection.close();
    });

  }
);
```

Call this one `addIndex.js` and execute it. Then, run the benchmark again. This is my result:

```
~$ time node query.js

[ { _id: 53d7955c3ac66b9e0af26745,  n: '#36271',  v:  6 },
  { _id: 53d7955c3ac66b9e0af26757,  n: '#36289',  v:  6 },
  { _id: 53d7955c3ac66b9e0af26761,  n: '#36299',  v:  6 },
  { _id: 53d7955c3ac66b9e0af2677a,  n: '#36324',  v:  6 },
  { _id: 53d7955c3ac66b9e0af2677b,  n: '#36325',  v:  6 },
  { _id: 53d7955c3ac66b9e0af26792,  n: '#36348',  v:  6 },
  { _id: 53d7955c3ac66b9e0af26794,  n: '#36350',  v:  6 },
  { _id: 53d7955c3ac66b9e0af267b2,  n: '#36380',  v:  6 },
  { _id: 53d7955c3ac66b9e0af267b3,  n: '#36381',  v:  6 },
  { _id: 53d7955c3ac66b9e0af267b6,  n: '#36384',  v:  6 } ]

real  0m0.269s
user  0m0.236s
sys   0m0.033s
```

From 1 second to 0.2 seconds – quite an improvement. This effect becomes more significant the larger the collection is. With a 2,000,000 documents collection, the query takes 5.6 seconds without an index and still only 0.2 seconds with an index on my machine.

Querying collections efficiently

When retrieving large result sets from a MongoDB collection, the same rule that applies to MySQL database result sets also applies here: reading the complete result set into our Node.js process at once isn't going to be efficient resource-wise. Handling a result array with 2,000,000 entries will eat a lot of memory no matter what. This is what the *toArray* method, which we used until now, does:

```
collection.find().toArray(function (err, documents) {
  // We now have one large documents array
});
```

What `collection.find()` returns is a so-called **cursor object**. It can be transformed into an array, which is very convenient, but when handling lots of documents, it's better to handle each one separately using the cursor's `each` method:

```
collection.find().each(function (err, document) {
  // We retrieve one document with each callback invocation
});
```

This way, the cursor object will invoke the callback function for each document in the query result set, which means that Node.js only needs to claim memory for one document at a time.

Thus, instead of:

```
collection.find().toArray(function (err, documents) {
  console.dir(documents);
});
```

we can do:

```
collection.find().each(function (err, document) {
  console.dir(document);
});
```

if we want to print a whole result set to the screen. The callback will be invoked with the document parameter set to null if the end of the result set has been reached – therefore, we can rewrite our doFind, doInsert, and doUpdate script like this:

```
'use strict';

var MongoClient = require('mongodb').MongoClient;

MongoClient.connect(
  'mongodb://127.0.0.1:27017/accounting',
  function (err, connection) {
    var collection = connection.collection('customers');

    var doFind = function (callback) {
      collection.find(
        {},
        {'sort': '_id'}
      ).each(function (err, document) {
        if (document === null) {
          callback();
        } else {
          console.dir(document);
        }
      });
    };

    var doInsert = function (i) {
      if (i < 20) {
        var value = Math.floor(Math.random() * 10);
        collection.insert(
          {'n': '#' + i, 'v': value},
          function (err, count) {
```

```
          doInsert(i + 1);
        });
      } else {
        console.log();
        console.log('Inserted', i, 'documents:');
        doFind(function () {
          doUpdate();
        });
      }
    };

    var doUpdate = function () {
      collection.update(
        {'n': /^#1/},
        {'$mul': {'v': 2} },
        {'multi': true},
        function (err, count) {
          console.log();
          console.log('Updated', count, 'documents:');
          doFind(function () {
            collection.remove({}, function () {
              connection.close();
            });
          });
        });
    };

    doInsert(0);

});
```

The mongodb driver also provides a convenient way to access the records of a result set through a streaming API. The following code excerpt shows a version of the doFind function which has been rewritten to make use of this API:

```
var doFind = function (callback) {

  var stream = collection.find(
    {},
    {'sort': '_id'}
  ).stream();

  stream.on('data', function(document) {
    console.dir(document);
  });

  stream.on('end', function() {
    callback();
```

```
    });

};
```

As you can see, it's quite simple: The `stream` method of the cursor object returned by `collection.find()` returns a stream object which emits `data` and `end` events, among others.

We can then attach callback functions to these events where we either print the incoming document, or call the provided callback function in order to continue our script.

 The stream object returned by `collection.find().stream()` implements the `stream.Readable` interface. See *the corresponding Node.js documentation chapter*(`https://nodejs.org/api/stream.html#stream_cl ass_stream_readable`) for more information.

Summary

In this chapter we learned about the workings of MongoDB and the `mongodb` driver, which enables us to insert, update, retrieve and remove documents from this NoSQL database. We learned about query filters and complex update operations, demonstrated how indexes can significantly accelerate query operations, and showed how to handle large result sets efficiently.

Part 2: Building a Complete Web Application with Node.js and Angular

Introduction

I want to admit it right away: Looking at the amount of code, this part is probably more about AngularJS than Node.js – but I think it's important to see how Node.js can be used as one part in a complete application. Also, I'm a huge fan of AngularJS and am firmly convinced that knowing Node.js and AngularJS in combination is extremely valuable.

Nevertheless, besides teaching you a bit about building AngularJS frontends, the chapter does teach you a lot about Node.js, too. We will learn how to create a full-fledged RESTful web service API, and probably even more important, we will learn how to do so in a fully test-driven manner using end-to-end test specifications.

Additionally, we will talk about using a database abstraction layer, and we will learn how to integrate database migrations into our development and testing workflow. All in all, we will learn a lot about creating Node.js applications for the real world.

 The code of the final application is also available at `https://github.com`
`/manuelkiessling/nodecraftsman/tree/master/ch10_building_a_com`
`plete_web_application_with_nodejs_and_angularjs`

The requirements from a user's perspective

What we are going to build is an application which allows its users to comfortably manage a set of structured data from the world of food and cooking.

The data basically is a collection of keywords like *Aubergine, Knife,* or *Paul Bocuse,* and these keywords are mapped into categories, like *Vegetable, Utility,* or *Famous chef.*

What's needed now is an application where users can browse and edit this data: create new keywords, delete keywords, change the value of existing keywords, and change the category of keywords. Thus, at the heart of it we need a CRUD application, with a little bit of extra functionality.

It has already been decided that the users want a web-based solution. The data will be stored in a relational database.

This is how the user interface will look like:

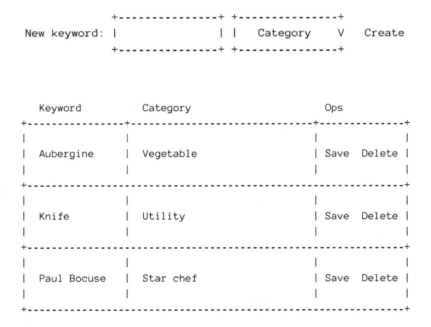

What this depicts is a screen with a table of keywords and the categories they are mapped to. Each row also has an operations column which allows to **Save** and **Delete** a keyword.

Above this table is a form which allows to **Create** a new keyword.

Being the JavaScript aficionados that we are, we are going to create the application as an AngularJS frontend that talks to a RESTful web service API on the backend written in Node.js.

High level architecture overview

The following is an overview about the most important architectonical parts of our application:

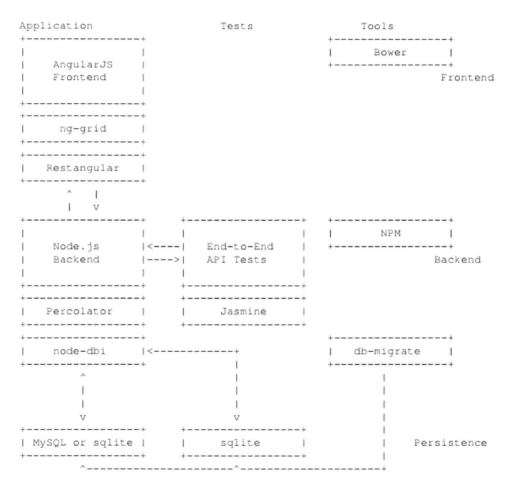

We will make use of the AngularJS plugin `Restangular` which will help us manage our web service calls.

Our backend server will be built using `Percolator`, a library which streamlines the creation of RESTful APIs with Node.js.

We are going to use different database solutions for testing & development (sqlite) and production (MySQL), which is why we will use `node-dbi`, a database access abstraction layer.

In order to ease database schema management in different environments, we will use the `db-migrate` tool that handles the details of versioning the structural changes of our project's database.

Once again *Jasmine* will be our testing framework – this time, however, we are going to create end-to-end tests instead of unit tests.

As always, *NPM* will be our trusty companion when it comes to dependency management on the backend –on the frontend side, *bower* will take that role.

Setting up the development environment

This is going to be our largest application to date, so let's make sure we can work comfortably.

Let's start by creating a project folder – let's call our project *Keyword Wrangler*:

```
$ mkdir keyword-wrangler
```

Next, we initialize a Node.js project in this folder by running `npm init` and answering the upcoming questions as follows:

```
$ npm init
```

This utility will walk you through creating a `package.json` file. It only covers the most common items, and tries to guess sane defaults:

```
See `npm help json` for definitive documentation on these fields
and exactly what they do.

Use `npm install <pkg> --save` afterwards to install a package and
save it as a dependency in the package.json file.

Press ^C at any time to quit.
name: (keyword-wrangler)
version: (1.0.0) 0.0.1
description: A tool to manage keywords
entry point: (index.js) src/backend/index.js
test command:
git repository:
keywords:
author:
license: (ISC)
About to write to keyword-wrangler/package.json:

{
   "name": "keyword-wrangler",
   "version": "0.0.1",
   "description": "A tool to manage keywords",
   "main": "src/backend/index.js",
   "scripts": {
     "test": "echo \"Error: no test specified\" && exit 1"
   },
   "author": "",
   "license": "ISC"
 }


Is this ok? (yes) yes
```

 Make sure to execute the `npm init` command *within* the keyword-wrangler folder!

This gives us a sensible `package.json` file to start with. We can now start to pull in all the dependencies we need.

We are going to need the following Node.js packages:

- `percolator` - that's the REST framework we are going to use
- `node-dbi` - an SQL abstraction layer
- `mysql` - The MySQL db driver, used by `node-dbi`
- `sqlite3` - The sqlite3 db driver, used by `node-dbi`
- `db-migrate` - an SQL migrations manager
- `async` - we are going to write some asynchronous orchestration
- `jasmine` - the test framework
- `request` - this enables us to talk to the API we will build from within our tests
- `bower` - the dependency and package manager for the frontend application

Running

```
$ npm install async@2.1.4 bower@1.8.0 db-migrate@0.9.26 mysql@2.12.0 \
node-dbi@0.7.1 percolator@1.5.0 --save
$ npm install jasmine-node@1.14.5 request@2.79.0 sqlite3@3.1.8 --save-dev
```

will install the listed versions of these packages and add them as dependencies to the `package.json` file. We only need *Jasmine* and *request* during development, which is why we install them separately with `--save-dev`. This allows to selectively install only the non-dev packages for production (per default, however, npm always installs all dependencies).

 The reason I'm asking you to install these exact versions of the dependencies is that it ensures that you will get a working setup, even if you are reading an older version of this book.

9
Milestone 1 – A First Passing Test against the Server

We will approach the requirements through a set of milestones. The first milestone we will try to reach is a very first passing end-to-end Jasmine test case against our web service API.

Let's see what we need to reach that milestone:

- We need to be able to execute Jasmine test cases
- We need a Jasmine spec that requests our HTTP backend
- We need an HTTP backend that responds to the request

In order to verify that we are good to go in regards to executing Jasmine test cases, let's create a subfolder spec/e2e in our project directory:

```
mkdir -p spec/e2e
```

Next, we create the file that will hold the end-to-end tests for our yet-to-be-written API server. We name it apiSpec.js and store it within the spec/e2e folder we just created:

```
'use strict';
describe('The API', function () {

  it('should just work', function () {
    expect(true).toBe(true);
  });

});
```

As long as the test infrastructure itself works correctly, this will of course pass. Let's verify that:

```
$ ./node_modules/.bin/jasmine-node --verbose ./spec/
The API - 1 ms
    should just work - 1 ms

Finished in 0.004 seconds
1 test, 1 assertion, 0 failures, 0 skipped
```

 The ./node_modules/.bin is a folder with shortcuts to all the executables within node_modules. The actual executable in this case is ./node_modules/jasmine-node/bin/jasmine-node

Ok, great, we can build on that. The goal of our first milestone is to have a test case which successfully requests a server backend and checks for the correct response. Let's rewrite apiSpec.js accordingly:

```
'use strict';

var request = require('request');

describe('The API', function () {

  it('should respond to a GET request at /api/keywords/', function
  (done) {
    request.get(
      {
        'url': 'http://localhost:8080/api/keywords/',
        'json': true
      },
      function (err, res, body) {
        expect(res.statusCode).toBe(200);
        expect(body.foo).toEqual('bar');
        done();
      });
  });

});
```

If we re-execute the test command, we get – nothing. Not only a failed test run, but literally no output to the console whatsoever. The problem is that there isn't any server yet that could respond to our GET request; however, *Jasmine* remains silent about that.

The reason is that requesting the missing HTTP server leads to an exception, and we need to explicitly tell *Jasmine* that we want to see exceptions:

```
$ ./node_modules/.bin/jasmine-node --verbose --captureExceptions ./spec/
TypeError: Cannot read property 'statusCode' of undefined
    at Request._callback (keyword-wrangler/spec/e2e/apiSpec.js:14:19)
    at self.callback (keyword-
wrangler/node_modules/request/request.js:373:22)
    at Request.emit (events.js:95:17)
    at Request.onRequestError (keyword- \
wrangler/node_modules/request/request.js:971:8)
    at ClientRequest.emit (events.js:95:17)
    at Socket.socketErrorListener (http.js:1552:9)
    at Socket.emit (events.js:95:17)
    at net.js:441:14
    at process._tickCallback (node.js:442:13)
```

Ok, it's time to create a web server. As said, we will use a library for this, namely `Percolator`. The `spec` we defined expects a server at port `8080` that responds with `{"foo": "bar"}` when receiving a `GET` request at `/api/keywords/`. Let's see how to implement this behaviour with `Percolator`.

Put the following into file `src/backend/index.js`:

```
'use strict';
var Percolator = require('percolator').Percolator;

var port = 8080;
var server = Percolator({'port': port});

server.route('/api/keywords',
  {
    GET: function (req, res) {
      res.object({'foo': 'bar'}).send()
    }
  }
);

server.listen(function() {
  console.log('Server started and listening on port', port);
});
```

Then, start this server in a new console window:

```
$ node src/backend/index.js
Server started and listening on port 8080
```

Now, running the `test` command again should look much better:

```
$ ./node_modules/.bin/jasmine-node --verbose --captureExceptions ./spec/
The API - 19 ms
   should respond to a GET request at /api/keywords/ - 18 ms

Finished in 0.021 seconds
1 test, 2 assertions, 0 failures, 0 skipped
```

Great, our first milestone has been reached.

Downloading the example code

You can download the example code files for this book from your account at
`http://www.packtpub.com`. The code bundle for the book is also hosted on GitHub at
`https://github.com/PacktPublishing/The-Node-Craftsman-Book`

10
Milestone 2 – The API Responds with Actual Database Content

Let's now look at how to integrate database access into our server application. We defined that within our local development and test environment, we would like to use *sqlite*. Let's start with this.

Abstracting database access

In order to connect to the database, we are going to use an abstraction layer by utilizing `node-dbi`. This allows us to transparently use **MySQL** at a later point in time, without the need to change the code that does database operations.

First, we should change our spec in order to have it expect actual database content. A request to `/api/keywords/` should return a JSON structure that carries an array of objects, where each object represents a keyword with its ID, value, and the ID of its category:

```
[
    {"id": 1, "value": "Aubergine", "categoryID": 1},
    {"id": 2, "value": "Onion", "categoryID": 1},
    {"id": 3, "value": "Knife", "categoryID": 2}
]
```

A data structure like this would be stored in a relational database like this:

```
Table: keyword
+-----------------------------------------------------------+
| id | value                                  | categoryID |
+===========================================================+
|  1 | Aubergine                              | 1          |
+-----------------------------------------------------------+
|  2 | Onion                                  | 1          |
+-----------------------------------------------------------+
|  3 | Knife                                  | 2          |
+-----------------------------------------------------------+
```

```
Table: category
+----------------------------------------------------------+
| id | name                                                |
+==========================================================+
|  1 | Vegetable                                           |
+----------------------------------------------------------+
|  2 | Utility                                             |
+----------------------------------------------------------+
```

 In this structure, `keyword.categoryID` is a foreign key to `category.id`. For now, however, we will only work with the `keyword` table.

Assuming the above example database content during a test run, our spec expectation needs to look like this (in file `spec/e2e/apiSpec.js`):

```
'use strict';
var request = require('request');

describe('The API', function () {

    it('should respond to a GET request at /api/keywords/', function
```

```
(done) {
  var expected = {
    "_items": [
      {'id': 1, 'value': 'Aubergine', 'categoryID': 1},
      {'id': 2, 'value': 'Onion', 'categoryID': 1},
      {'id': 3, 'value': 'Knife', 'categoryID': 2}
    ]
  };

  request.get(
    {
      'url': 'http://localhost:8080/api/keywords/',
      'json': true
    },
    function (err, res, body) {
      expect(res.statusCode).toBe(200);
      expect(body).toEqual(expected);
      done();
    });
});

});
```

 Note how `expected` is an object with a field `_items`, which contains the actual list of keywords. The `Percolator` library doesn't allow to return an array of things directly.

There is still some work to do in order to make this succeed.

Ensuring a clean slate for test runs

We are going to make our lives a lot easier if we write some helper code for our tests which ensures that at the start of each test run, the database is empty. Let's put this into `spec/resetDatabase.js`:

```
'use strict';
var async = require('async');

var resetDatabase = function (dbSession, callback) {

  async.series(
    [

      function (callback) {
```

```
      dbSession.remove('keyword', '1', function (err) {
        callback(err)
      });
    },

    function (callback) {
      dbSession.remove('category', '1', function (err) {
        callback(err)
      });
    }

  ],

  function (err, results) {
    callback(err);
  }
);

};

module.exports = resetDatabase;
```

As you can see, we make use of a dbSession object. We need to create a module where this is set up, in file src/backend/dbSession.js:

```
'use strict';
var DBWrapper = require('node-dbi').DBWrapper;

var dbWrapper = new DBWrapper('sqlite3', {'path': '/var/tmp/keyword\
-wrangler.test.sqlite'});
dbWrapper.connect();
module.exports = dbWrapper;
```

 This is a very simplistic implementation – we will later refine it in order to allow for different database setups depending on the environment.

Let's now create the sqlite database file with the keyword and category table:

```
$ sqlite3 /var/tmp/keyword-wrangler.test.sqlite
sqlite> CREATE TABLE keyword (id INTEGER PRIMARY KEY, value TEXT,
categoryID INTEGER);
sqlite> CREATE TABLE category (id INTEGER PRIMARY KEY, name TEXT);
sqlite> .quit
```

Install the `sqlite3` package if it is not available on your system!

Completing the first spec

We now have the boilerplate code and database structures needed to further complete our spec:

```
'use strict';
var request = require('request');
var dbSession = require('../../src/backend/dbSession.js');
var resetDatabase = require('../resetDatabase.js');
var async = require('async');

describe('The API', function () {

  it('should respond to a GET request at /api/keywords/', function
  (done) {
    var expected = {
      "_items": [
        {'id': 1, 'value': 'Aubergine', 'categoryID': 1},
        {'id': 2, 'value': 'Onion', 'categoryID': 1},
        {'id': 3, 'value': 'Knife', 'categoryID': 2}
      ]
    };

    async.series(
      [

        function(callback) {
          resetDatabase(dbSession, callback);
        },

        function(callback) {
          dbSession.insert(
            'keyword',
            {'value': 'Aubergine', 'categoryID': 1},
            function(err) { callback(err) });
        },

        function(callback) {
          dbSession.insert(
            'keyword',
```

```
            {'value': 'Onion', 'categoryID': 1},
            function(err) { callback(err) });
        },

      function(callback) {
        dbSession.insert(
          'keyword',
          {'value': 'Knife', 'categoryID': 2},
          function(err) { callback(err) });
        }

    ],

    function(err, results) {
      request.get(
        {
          'url': 'http://localhost:8080/api/keywords/',
          'json': true
        },
        function (err, res, body) {
          expect(res.statusCode).toBe(200);
          expect(body).toEqual(expected);
          done();
        }
      );
    }

  );

});

});
```

With this, our spec is complete – we empty the database, insert our test data, and expect the web service API to respond with the data we just inserted. This is not yet the behavior of the API – we need to rewrite `src/backend/index.js`:

```
'use strict';
var Percolator = require('percolator').Percolator;
var dbSession = require('../../src/backend/dbSession.js');

var port = 8080;
var server = Percolator({'port': port, 'autoLink': false});

server.route('/api/keywords',
  {
    GET: function (req, res) {
      dbSession.fetchAll('SELECT id, value, categoryID FROM keyword \
```

```
      ORDER BY id', function(err, rows) {
        if (err) {
          console.log(err);
          res.status.internalServerError(err);
        } else {
          res.collection(rows).send();
        }
      });
    }
  }
);

server.listen(function() {
  console.log('Server started and listening on port', port);
});
```

 Don't forget to restart the server after making changes to it!

Our tests now pass again, and thus our second milestone has been reached.

11
Milestone 3 – Setting the Stage for a Continuous Delivery Workflow

We are already growing our application driven by tests, however, there are still some inconveniences that hinder us from going fully continuous. If the goal is to put every change we make into production automatically (safeguarded by our tests, of course), then we need to automate the things we still do manually: starting the server and changing the database structure.

Let's tackle the server startup first. It would be great if each test case would start and stop the server process as needed. This is possible by refactoring the server code a bit.

We need to split into two files what is currently handled in `src/backend/index.js`. The goal here is to have the server **logic** in one file, and the server **startup** in another one. This way, our tests can start the server logic up by themselves, and for production, we still have a file we can execute.

To achieve this, let's create a file `src/backend/server.js` with the following content:

```
'use strict';
var Percolator = require('percolator').Percolator;
var dbSession = require('../../src/backend/dbSession.js');

var Server = function(port) {
  var server = Percolator({'port': port, 'autoLink': false});

  server.route('/api/keywords',
  {
```

```
    GET: function (req, res) {
      dbSession.fetchAll('SELECT id, value, categoryID FROM keyword \
      ORDER BY id',
      function(err, rows) {
        if (err) {
          console.log(err);
          res.status.internalServerError(err);
        } else {
          res.collection(rows).send();
        }
      });
    }
  }
);
return server;
};

module.exports = {'Server': Server};
```

This isn't that much different from what we had in `index.js` until now. But instead of configuring the server and starting it up directly, we now merely provide a `Server` function that sets up a `Percolator` server object for us. It's then our business to get that server going – we do so in `src/backend/index.js`:

```
'use strict';
var Server = require('./server.js').Server;
var server = Server('8080');

server.listen(function() {
  console.log('Server started and listening on port', server.options.port);
});
```

This way, we can still start the server via node `src/backend/index.js`. However, we can now also manage the server from other parts of our code – for example, from our tests in `spec/e2e/apiSpec.js`.

```
'use strict';
var request = require('request');
var dbSession = require('../../src/backend/dbSession.js');
var Server = require('../../src/backend/server.js').Server;
var resetDatabase = require('../resetDatabase.js');
var async = require('async');

describe('The API', function () {

  var server;
```

```
beforeEach(function (done) {
  server = Server('8081');
  server.listen(function (err) {
    resetDatabase(dbSession, function() {
      done(err);
    });
  });
});

afterEach(function (done) {
  server.close(function () {
    resetDatabase(dbSession, function() {
      done();
    });
  });
});

it('should respond to a GET request at /api/keywords/', function
(done) {
  var expected = {
    "_items": [
      {'id': 1, 'value': 'Aubergine', 'categoryID': 1},
      {'id': 2, 'value': 'Onion', 'categoryID': 1},
      {'id': 3, 'value': 'Knife', 'categoryID': 2}
    ]
  };

  async.series(
    [

      function(callback) {
        dbSession.insert(
          'keyword',
          {'value': 'Aubergine', 'categoryID': 1},
          function(err) { callback(err) });
      },

      function(callback) {
        dbSession.insert(
          'keyword',
          {'value': 'Onion', 'categoryID': 1},
          function(err) { callback(err) });
      },

      function(callback) {
        dbSession.insert(
          'keyword',
          {'value': 'Knife', 'categoryID': 2},
```

```
              function(err) { callback(err) });
          }

      ],

      function(err, results) {
        if (err) throw(err);
        request.get(
        {
            'url': 'http://localhost:8081/api/keywords/',
            'json': true
        },
        function (err, res, body) {
          expect(res.statusCode).toBe(200);
          expect(body).toEqual(expected);
          done();
        }
      );
    }

  );

});

});
```

Now, our specs no longer require an already running server: **before each** test case, the server is started, and **after each** case, it is shut down. We also moved the database reset step into these blocks.

Also, we are now using port 8081 for our tests, versus port 8080 which is used for production (do not forget to change the port in the `server = Server( '8081' );` line).

With this, you can now stop the running server, and you can execute test runs without the need to start the server.

Introducing automatic database migrations

Let's take the final step in automation by setting up database migrations. A migration is a change to the database structure of our application. For example, if we change our code and it now expects a new field in one of our tables, the migration would be the code that alters the table structure and adds the missing field. Making these migrations part of our code base allows us to automate this – when the tests or the application is started, all migrations that are not yet applied to the database are applied automatically; we no longer need to ensure manually that our code and our database structures are in sync.

The Node.js module that takes care of this for us is `db-migrate`. We already installed it via `npm`.

This modules expects a `database.json` file where it can find the database connection parameters for different environments. An environment is, for example, `test`, or `production`. This way, we can use different database configurations for our different environments. We declared that we would like to use `sqlite` for our tests and `MySQL` in production; the `database.json` file makes this kind of setup simple (and, as we will see, we can use it for `db-migrate` and from our own code).

Here is the `database.json` file we need:

```
{
  "test": {
    "driver": "sqlite3",
    "filename": "/var/tmp/keyword-wrangler.test.sqlite"
  },
  "dev": {
    "driver": "sqlite3",
    "filename": "/var/tmp/keyword-wrangler.dev.sqlite"
  },

  "production": {
    "driver": "mysql",
    "host": "localhost",
    "user": "root",
    "password": "root",
    "database": "keyword_wrangler"
  }
}
```

The file needs to reside in the root folder of our project.

We also need a place for our migrations. By default, the migration files are placed in a folder called `migrations`, again in the root folder of our project.

We can now create our first migration; it will programmatically create the `keyword` and `category` tables we already created manually. Migrations are files with JavaScript code, but we don't need to create them manually. The `db-migrate` file does this for us:

```
$ ./node_modules/.bin/db-migrate create createKeywordAndCategoryTable --env
test
```

This gives you a file with a name like `migrations/20150127080251-createKeywordAndCategoryTable.js` and the following content:

```
var dbm = require('db-migrate');
var type = dbm.dataType;

exports.up = function(db, callback) {

};

exports.down = function(db, callback) {

};
```

Two functions, one up, one down. The up function carries the code that is to be executed if a migration needs to be applied. The down function carries the reverse, that is, the code that is needed to un-apply or rollback the migration.

Given our database structure, here is how this looks in practice:

```
'use strict';
var dbm = require('db-migrate');
var type = dbm.dataType;
var async = require('async');

exports.up = function(db, callback) {
  async.series(
    [

      db.createTable.bind(db, 'keyword', {
        id: { type: 'int', primaryKey: true, autoIncrement: true, \
        notNull: true },
        value: { type: 'string', length: '128', notNull: true, unique: \
        true },
        categoryID: { type: 'int', notNull: true }
      }),

      db.createTable.bind(db, 'category', {
        id: { type: 'int', primaryKey: true, autoIncrement: true, \
        notNull: true },
```

```
        name: { type: 'string', length: '128', notNull: true }
      })

  ], callback);
};

exports.down = function(db, callback) {
  async.series(
    [
      db.dropTable.bind(db, 'keyword'),
      db.dropTable.bind(db, 'category')
    ], callback);
};
```

The up step will create our tables, the down step will remove them. This is the equivalent of the manual SQL operations we did earlier. And because we already did that manually, we need to remove them before our migrations can work. The most simple way to do this is by deleting the sqlite database file:

```
$ rm /var/tmp/keyword-wrangler.test.sqlite
```

We are now able to run our migrations:

```
$ ./node_modules/.bin/db-migrate up --env test
[INFO] Processed migration 20150127080251-createKeywordAndCategoryTable
[INFO] Done
```

Looks good. This creates the tables, and additionally creates a table named migrations, where db-migrate keeps track of the migrations already applied:

```
$ sqlite3 /var/tmp/keyword-wrangler.test.sqlite
sqlite> SELECT * FROM migrations;

1|20150127080251-createKeywordAndCategoryTable|1422435911741
```

So, from now on we need to combine our migration runs with our test runs; whenever we change the code and its tests in a way that makes them expect a different database structure, we need to create a new migrations file, program the required database changes into them, and can then apply them, followed by a test run:

```
$ ./node_modules/.bin/db-migrate up --env test && \
  ./node_modules/.bin/jasmine-node --verbose --captureExceptions
  ./spec/
```

The great thing is that now all development steps can be automatized, and we can ensure that code and database are always in sync. Imagine that another developer clones the repository with your code. Given that she has a working Node.js environment, all she needs to do is:

- check out the code
- run `npm install`
- run the migrations

and she is immediately up-to-date with her development environment for your project.

Milestone 3 has been reached!

12
Milestone 4 – Giving Users a Frontend

We have now reached a point where our backend service deserves a frontend. As said, we want this to be based on AngularJS. Furthermore, we will use the `Restangular` library (which will ease the communication with our backend web service), and `ngGrid`, which makes building dynamic tables straightforward.

Setting up frontend dependencies through bower

The very first step is to utilize `Bower`, the package manager for frontend JavaScript projects, to pull in the dependencies of our project.

We need to create a directory `src/frontend`, and place a `bower.json` file into it with the following contents:

```
{
    "name": "keyword-wrangler-client",
    "dependencies": {
      "angular": "1.3.15",
      "angular-route": "1.3.15",
      "angular-grid": "2.0.14",
      "restangular": "1.4.0",
      "bootstrap": "3.3.4", "async": "0.9.2"
    }, "analytics": false
}
```

Then, while in folder `keyword-wrangler/src/frontend`, run:

```
$ ../../node_modules/.bin/bower install
```

This will install all dependencies into `src/frontend/bower_components`.

Serving the frontend through the backend server

Before we start building our frontend app, let's make sure we can browse to it.

To do so, change the `"restangular" : "1.4.0"` , line in `src/backend/server.js`:

```
var server = Percolator({'port': port, 'autoLink': false});
```

The changed line is as follows:

```
var server = Percolator({'port': port, 'autoLink': false, 'staticDir':\
__dirname + '/../frontend'});
```

With this change, `Percolator` will serve everything in `src/frontend` as static files (while still serving the API at the `/api` route).

Adding the frontend code

Time to start building the app. Create `src/frontend/index.html` as follows:

```html
<!DOCTYPE html>
< html ng-app="app" >

  <head>
    <meta charset="UTF-8"/>
    <title>Keyword Wrangler</title>

    <link rel="stylesheet" \
    href="bower_components/bootstrap/dist/css/bootstrap.css">
    <link rel="stylesheet" href="bower_components/angular-grid/ng-\
    grid.min.css">
    <style>
      .gridStyle {
        margin-top: 20px;
        height: 800px;
```

```
      }
    </style>
  </head>

  <body>
    <div id="main" class="container">
      <div class="span12" ng-view></div>
    </div>

    <script src="bower_components/async/lib/async.js"></script>
    <script src="bower_components/jquery/dist/jquery.js"></script>
    <script src="bower_components/lodash/dist/lodash.js"></script>
    <script src="bower_components/angular/angular.js"></script>
    <script src="bower_components/angular-route/angular-route.js">
    </script>
    <script src="bower_components/restangular/dist/restangular.js">
    </script>
    <script src="bower_components/angular-grid/build/ng-grid.js">
    </script>

    <script src="app/app.js"></script>
    <script src="app/lib/resolveEntity.js"></script>
    <script src="app/lib/RepositoryFactory.js"></script>
    <script src="app/keywords/KeywordsController.js"></script>
  </body>

</html>
```

When running the backend server locally, this will be served at
`http://localhost:8080/`, and will host our single-page app.

As you can see in the `<script src="app/app.js" ></script>` line and following, we
need to provide several JavaScript files – these are the components of our AngularJS
application.

Let's start with `src/frontend/app/app.js`:

```
'use strict';

(function() {

  var app = angular.module('app', ['ngRoute', 'ngGrid', 'restangular']);

  app.config(['$routeProvider',
  function($routeProvider) {

    // This makes app/keywords/KeywordsController.js handle the \
    http://localhost:8080/#/ URL
```

```
$routeProvider.
  when('/', {
    templateUrl: 'app/keywords/partials/editor.html',
    controller: 'KeywordsController'
  });

}]);

})();
```

This defines the main entry point for the AngularJS applications. It sets up dependencies and in-app routing.

The key component here is the `KeywordController`. Put this into `src/frontend/app/keywords/KeywordsController.js`:

```
'use strict';
(function() {

  var app = angular.module('app');

  app.controller('KeywordsController', function($scope, \
  RepositoryFactory, resolveEntity) {

    /* == Frontend Initialization == */

    /* All of this happens as soon as the page loads */

    /* resolveEntity is a helper function which is used in \
    partials/keywordCategoryGridCell.html in order to display the name
    of a keyword category based on its id */
    $scope.resolveEntity = resolveEntity;

    /* A repository is the connection between this controller and the
    REST Api. We use one for keyword categories... */
    var KeywordCategoriesRepository = new RepositoryFactory({
      endpoint: 'keywords/categories',
      retrieveItems: function (data) {
        return data._items;
      }
    });

    /* ...and one for keywords */
    var KeywordsRepository = new RepositoryFactory({
      endpoint: 'keywords',
      retrieveItems: function(data) {
        return data._items;
      }
```

```
  });

  /* When the frontend loads, we want the controller to immediately
   load all keyword categories and categories from the API */
  KeywordCategoriesRepository.readAll().then(function(keywordCategories)
{
  $scope.keywordCategories = keywordCategories;
  KeywordsRepository.readAll().then(function(keywords) {
    $scope.keywords = keywords;
  });
});

  /* The grid. This part is best coded while listening to the Tron: \
   Legacy soundtrack. */
  $scope.keywordsGridOptions = {
    data: 'keywords', // This makes the grid use the data in
    $scope.keywords
    enableCellSelection: false, // breaks edit of cells with select\
    element if true
    enableCellEdit: true,
    keepLastSelected: false,
    enableRowSelection: false,
    multiSelect: false,
    enableSorting: true,
    enableColumnResize: true,
    enableColumnReordering: true,
    showFilter: false,
    rowHeight: '40',
    columnDefs: [
      {
        field: 'id',
        displayName: 'ID',
        enableCellEdit: false,
        width: '80px'
      },
      {
        field: 'value',
        displayName: 'Value'
      },
      {
        /* The keyword category field does not use the build-in\
         cell template, but our own */
         field: 'keywordCategoryID',
         displayName: 'Category',
         cellTemplate:
         'app/keywords/partials/keywordCategoryGridCell.html',
         editableCellTemplate: 'app/keywords/partials\
         /keywordCategoryGridCellEditor.html'
```

```
      },
      {
         /* Same goes for the operations column */
         field: '',
         displayName: 'Operations',
         cellTemplate:
         'app/keywords/partials/operationsGridCell.html',
         enableCellEdit: false,
         sortable: false
      }
   ]
};


/* == Frontend Operations == */

/* These functions are called when the frontend is operated, for \
   example, if a button is clicked */

   $scope.createKeyword = function(newKeyword) {
     $scope.$broadcast('ngGridEventEndCellEdit');
     if (newKeyword.value.length > 0) {
       KeywordsRepository.createOne(newKeyword).then(function ()
       {
         KeywordsRepository.readAll().then(function (keywords) {
           $scope.keywords = keywords;
         });
       });
     }
   };

   $scope.updateKeyword = function(keyword) {
     $scope.$broadcast('ngGridEventEndCellEdit');
     KeywordsRepository.updateOne(keyword);
   };

   $scope.deleteKeyword = function(keyword) {
     $scope.$broadcast('ngGridEventEndCellEdit');
     KeywordsRepository.deleteOne(keyword).then(function() {
       KeywordsRepository.readAll().then(function(keywords) {
         $scope.keywords = keywords;
       });
     });
   };

/* These are here to make the grid behave cleanly in regards to \
   the keyword category select */
   $scope.stopEditingKeywordCategory = function() {
```

```
            $scope.$broadcast('ngGridEventEndCellEdit');
        };

        $scope.$on('ngGridEventRows', function(newRows) {
          $scope.$broadcast('ngGridEventEndCellEdit');
        });

      });

  })();
```

This controller has two dependencies, `RepositoryFactory` and `resolveEntity`. Let's define those.

In file `src/frontend/app/lib/RepositoryFactory.js`:

```
'use strict';
(function() {

  var app = angular.module('app');

  app.factory(
    'RepositoryFactory',
    ['Restangular', '$q', RepositoryFactory]
  );

  function RepositoryFactory(Restangular, $q) {

    Restangular.setBaseUrl('/api/');

    var Repository = function(options) {
      this.endpoint = options.endpoint;
      this.retrieveItems = options.retrieveItems;
    };

    Repository.prototype.readAll = function() {
      var self = this;
      var deferred = $q.defer();
      Restangular.all(self.endpoint + '/').doGET().then(function(data)
      {
          var items = self.retrieveItems(data);
          deferred.resolve(items);
      });
      return deferred.promise;
    };

     Repository.prototype.createOne = function(newItem) {
       var self = this;
```

```
        var deferred = $q.defer();
        Restangular.one(self.endpoint + '/', \
        '').post('',newItem).then(function(response)
    {
        deferred.resolve(response);
        });
        return deferred.promise;
    };

    Repository.prototype.updateOne = function(item) {
      var self = this;
      var deferred = $q.defer();
      Restangular.one(self.endpoint, item.id).post('', \
      item).then(function(response)
      {
          deferred.resolve(response);
        });
        return deferred.promise;
    };

    Repository.prototype.deleteOne = function(item) {
      var self = this;
      var deferred = $q.defer();
      Restangular.one(self.endpoint,
      item.id).remove().then(function(response) {
        deferred.resolve(response);
        });
        return deferred.promise;
    };

    return Repository;

  }

})();
```

This is basically a convenience wrapper for all the different API operations we are going to need for keywords and keyword categories: Reading, creating, updating, deleting, and merging.

Note how each operation is asynchronous and therefore returns promises. You can see how these operations are used in the controller throughout the code.

Of course, the web service routing and logic for these operations does not yet exist in our backend server (with the exception of `GET /api/keywords`. We will implement those soon.

We also need to create `src/frontend/app/lib/resolveEntity.js`, which is a helper function that is needed to get from category IDs to category names in the view of our app:

```
'use strict';
(function() {

  var app = angular.module('app');

  app.factory(
    'resolveEntity',
    [resolveEntity]
  );

  function resolveEntity() {

    return function(queryParams) {
      for (var i=0; i < queryParams.from.length; i++) {
        if (queryParams.from[i][queryParams.where] === queryParams.is)
        {
          return queryParams.from[i][queryParams.what];
        }
      }
      return false;
    };

  }

})();
```

Adding AngularJS view templates

With this, the JavaScript code for our AngularJS app is in place, but we aren't done yet. We also need four HTML views for the app: The main view with the editor, plus three custom grid cell templates, one for the operations column that holds the Save and Delete controls, one for the Category column cells (because there we need to translate from category IDs to category names), and one for the Category cells in edit mode, because when we edit the category of a keyword, we don't want to edit its name as a string, but rather choose from a list of existing categories through a dropdown control.

We start with `src/frontend/app/keywords/partials/editor.html`:

```
< div class="span12" >
 <form>
    <input
      class="input-medium"
      ng-model="newKeyword.value"
      ng-init="newKeyword.value = ''"
      type="text"
      placeholder="Name of new keyword"
      >
    <select
      ng-model="newKeyword.categoryID"
      ng-init="newKeyword.categoryID = 1"
      ng-options="keywordCategory.id as keywordCategory.name \
      for keywordCategory in keywordCategories" >
    </select>
    <button ng-class="newKeyword.value.length > 0 && 'btn \
   btn-success' || 'btn'" ng-click="newKeyword.value.length > 0 && \
   createKeyword(newKeyword) ">Create</button>
  </form>
</div>
<div class="gridStyle" ng-grid="keywordsGridOptions"></div>
```

This provides us with the form for creating new keywords, plus it provides the `div` element where `ngGrid` will render the table. Note how the `createKeyword` method of our `KeywordsController` is called upon clicking the **Create** button.

Now we create `src/frontend/app/keywords/partials/operationsGridCell.html`:

```
< button class="btn btn-primary" ng-click="updateKeyword(row.entity)" \
>Save</button>
< button class="btn btn-warning" ng-click="deleteKeyword(row.entity)" \
>Delete</button>
```

These buttons simply call the according controller methods, passing the keyword entity of the according row as a parameter.

We can now create the HTML template for the grid cells displaying the category name of a keyword, in file
`src/frontend/app/keywords/partials/keywordCategoryGridCell.html`:

```
<div class="ngCellText" ng-class="col.colIndex()">
  <span ng-cell-text>
    {{
        resolveEntity(
          {
            'what' : 'name',
            'from' : keywordCategories,
            'where' : 'id',
            'is' : row.entity.categoryID
          }
        );
    }}
  </span>
</div>
```

This makes use of the helper function we created earlier.

Last but not least, we need a custom grid cell template for editing the category of a keyword, in file
`src/frontend/app/keywords/partials/keywordCategoryGridCellEditor.html`:

```
<select
  class="form-control"
  ng-model ="row.entity.categoryID"
  ng-options="keywordCategory.id as keywordCategory.name for \
  keywordCategory in keywordCategories"
  ng-blur="stopEditingTagHeading()" >
</select>
```

With this, all components of our frontend app are in place, and we could give it a try in our browser. But not yet, because the backend still needs a lot of changes.

13
Milestone 5 – More Work on the Backend

Adding a route for retrieving categories

We currently only provide keywords data through our backend API. The app requests keywords data as well as categories data, and the latter would fail for now. Let's implement the required route and logic now.

We first need to extend the spec in `spec/e2e/apiSpec.js`:

```
'use strict';
var request = require('request');
var dbSession = require('../../src/backend/dbSession.js');
var Server = require('../../src/backend/server.js').Server;
var resetDatabase = require('../resetDatabase.js');
var async = require('async');

describe('The API', function () {

  var server;

  beforeEach(function (done) {
    server = Server('8081');
    server.listen(function (err) {
      resetDatabase(dbSession, function() {
        done(err);
      });
    });
  });
```

```
afterEach(function (done) {
  server.close(function () {
    resetDatabase(dbSession, function() {
      done();
    });
  });
});


it('should respond to a GET request at /api/keywords/', function \
(done)
{
  var expected = {
    "_items": [
      {'id': 1, 'value': 'Aubergine', 'categoryID': 1},
      {'id': 2, 'value': 'Onion', 'categoryID': 1},
      {'id': 3, 'value': 'Knife', 'categoryID': 2}
    ]
  };

  async.series(
    [

      function(callback) {
        resetDatabase(dbSession, callback);
      },

      function(callback) {
        dbSession.insert(
          'keyword',
          {'value': 'Aubergine', 'categoryID': 1},
          function(err) { callback(err) });
      },

      function(callback) {
        dbSession.insert(
        'keyword',
        {'value': 'Onion', 'categoryID': 1},
        function(err) { callback(err) });
      },

      function(callback) {
        dbSession.insert(
          'keyword',
          {'value': 'Knife', 'categoryID': 2},
          function(err) { callback(err) });
      }
```

```
          ],

        function(err, results) {
          if (err) throw(err);
          request.get(
          {
            'url': 'http://localhost:8081/api/keywords/',
            'json': true
          },
          function (err, res, body) {
            expect(res.statusCode).toBe(200);
            expect(body).toEqual(expected);
            done();
          }
        );
      }

    );

  });


  it('should respond to a GET request at /api/keywords/categories/',
  function (done) {
    var expected = {
      "_items": [
        {'id': 1, 'name': 'Vegetable'},
        {'id': 2, 'name': 'Utility'}
      ]
    };

    async.series(
      [

        function(callback) {
          resetDatabase(dbSession, callback);
        },

        function(callback) {
          dbSession.insert(
            'category',
            {'name': 'Vegetable'},
            function(err) { callback(err) });
        },

        function(callback) {
          dbSession.insert(
            'category',
```

```
          {'name': 'Utility'},
          function(err) { callback(err) });
      }

    ],

    function(err, results) {
      if (err) throw(err);
      request.get(
        {
          'url': 'http://localhost:8081/api/keywords/categories/',
          'json': true
        },
        function (err, res, body) {
          expect(res.statusCode).toBe(200);
          expect(body).toEqual(expected);
          done();
        }
      );
    }

  );

});

});
```

Additional code is added after the `function(err, results)` function. In order to fulfill the new expectation, we need to extend `src/backend/server.js` as follows:

```
'use strict';
var Percolator = require('percolator').Percolator;
var dbSession = require('../../src/backend/dbSession.js');

var Server = function(port) {
  var server = Percolator({'port': port, 'autoLink': false, \
  'staticDir': __dirname + '/../frontend'});

  server.route('/api/keywords',
  {
    GET: function (req, res) {
      dbSession.fetchAll('SELECT id, value, categoryID FROM keyword \
      ORDER BY id', function(err, rows) {
        if (err) {
          console.log(err);
          res.status.internalServerError(err);
        } else {
          res.collection(rows).send();
```

```
        }
      });
    }
  }
);

server.route('/api/keywords/categories',
  {
    GET: function (req, res) {
      dbSession.fetchAll('SELECT id, name FROM category ORDER BY \
      id',
      function(err, rows) {
        if (err) {
          console.log(err);
          res.status.internalServerError(err);
        } else {
          res.collection(rows).send();
        }
      });
    }
  }
);

  return server;
};

module.exports = {'Server': Server};
```

One caveat: We also need to extend the resetDatabase helper in order to ensure that SQLite primary key sequencing is resetted for each test case:

```
'use strict';
var async = require('async');

var resetDatabase = function (dbSession, callback) {

  async.series(
    [

      function (callback) {
        dbSession.remove('keyword', '1', function (err) {
          callback(err)
        });
      },

      function (callback) {
        dbSession.remove('category', '1', function (err) {
          callback(err)
```

```
        });
      },

      function (callback) {
        dbSession.remove('sqlite_sequence', '1', function (err) {
          callback(err)
        });
      }

    ],

    function (err, results) {
      callback(err);
    }
  );

};

module.exports = resetDatabase;
```

We can now run the following command:

```
$ ./node_modules/.bin/jasmine-node --verbose --captureExceptions ./spec/
```

from the top folder of the project in order to verify that the new route behaves as expected.

Making the backend recognize different environments

But we are not yet done and need to refrain from opening our app just yet.

What's the problem?

Until now, we only used the database when running the specs. Now we have another client for the web service (and the underlying database), and this is the frontend application. We probably don't want our specs to wipe out the data we add through the application. We can circumvent this problem by using the different environments we created for `db-migrate`. Each environment has its own database setup, and this way we can keep things neatly separated – our specs work with one database setup, and the application with another one.

We need to add a helper script that detects the current environment when executing our code. Place this into `src/backend/env.js`:

```
'use strict';
```

```
(function() {
  var env;

  if (process.env.KW_ENV) {
    env = process.env.KW_ENV;
  } else {
    env = 'test';
  }

  if (!( env === 'test'
      || env === 'dev'
      || env === 'production')) {
    throw new Error('"' + env + '" is not an allowed environment');
  }

  module.exports = env;
})();
```

This will detect the environment based on a shell environment variable named KW_ENV. If no environment parameter can be detected, then the fallback is to assume the test environment.

Next, we need to make the database connection logic aware of the environment, and make it use the matching database connection configuration. We therefore need to change src/backend/dbSession.js as follows:

```
'use strict';
var env = require('./env');
var dbOptions = require('../../database.json')[env];
var DBWrapper = require('node-dbi').DBWrapper;

var dbWrapper;
if (dbOptions.driver === 'sqlite3') {
  var dbWrapper = new DBWrapper('sqlite3', {'path': dbOptions.filename});
} else if (dbOptions.driver === 'mysql') {
  dbWrapper = new DBWrapper('mysql', {
    'host': dbOptions.host,
    'user': dbOptions.user,
    'password': dbOptions.password,
    'database': dbOptions.database
  });
} else {
  throw(new Error('No suitable database config found.'));
}

dbWrapper.connect();
module.exports = dbWrapper;
```

We also need to make our `resetDatabase.js` helper in folder `spec` aware of the current environment, and make it handle each database type correctly:

```
'use strict';
var async = require('async');
var env = require('../src/backend/env');
var dbOptions = require('../database.json')[env];

var resetDatabase = function (dbSession, callback) {

  if (dbOptions.driver === 'sqlite3') {

    async.series(
      [

        function (callback) {
          dbSession.remove('keyword', '1', function (err) {
            callback(err)
          });
        },

        function (callback) {
          dbSession.remove('category', '1', function (err) {
            callback(err)
          });
        },

        function (callback) {
          dbSession.remove('sqlite_sequence', '1', function (err) {
            callback(err, null);
          });
        }

      ],

      function (err, results) {
        callback(err);
      }
    );

  }

  if (dbOptions.driver === 'mysql') {

    async.series(
      [

        function (callback) {
```

```
      dbSession.query('TRUNCATE keyword', [], function (err) {
        callback(err)
      });
    },

    function (callback) {
      dbSession.query('TRUNCATE category', [], function (err) {
        callback(err)
      });
    }

  ],

  function (err, results) {
    callback(err);
  }
);


  }

};

module.exports = resetDatabase;
```

We are now able to execute the specs as well as the server process under different environments:

```
# Apply migrations in dev environment
$ ./node_modules/.bin/db-migrate up --env dev

# Apply migrations in test environment
$ ./node_modules/.bin/db-migrate up --env test

# Run specs in dev environment
$ KW_ENV=dev ./node_modules/.bin/jasmine-node --verbose -- \
captureExceptions ./spec/

# Run specs in test environment
$ KW_ENV=test ./node_modules/.bin/jasmine-node --verbose \
--captureExceptions ./spec/

# Start server in dev environment
$ KW_ENV=dev node src/backend/index.js

# Start server in test environment
$ KW_ENV=test node src/backend/index.js
```

This shows how `db-migrate` supports environment detection based on the `-env` parameter, while our specs and our server make use of the `KW_ENV` variable.

We now have the backend and frontend code in place, we are able to run the backend server with a database config different from our specs runs – what's missing is some data to play around with in the `dev` environment. To fix this, simply run the following on the command line:

```
rm -f /var/tmp/keyword-wrangler.dev.sqlite
./node_modules/.bin/db-migrate up --env dev
echo "DELETE FROM category;" | sqlite3 /var/tmp/keyword-wrangler.dev.sqlite
echo "DELETE FROM keyword;" | sqlite3 /var/tmp/keyword-wrangler.dev.sqlite
echo "DELETE FROM sqlite_sequence;" | sqlite3 /var/tmp/keyword\
-wrangler.dev.sqlite
echo "INSERT INTO category (name) VALUES ('Vegetable');" | sqlite3 \
/var/tmp/keywordwrangler.dev.sqlite
echo "INSERT INTO category (name) VALUES ('Utility');" | sqlite3 \
/var/tmp/keyword-wrangler.dev.sqlite
echo "INSERT INTO keyword (value, categoryID) VALUES ('Aubergine', 1);" |
sqlite3 /var/tmp/keyword-wrangler.dev.sqlite
echo "INSERT INTO keyword (value, categoryID) VALUES ('Onion', 1);" | \
sqlite3 /var/tmp/keyword-wrangler.dev.sqlite
echo "INSERT INTO keyword (value, categoryID) VALUES ('Knife', 2);" | \
sqlite3 /var/tmp/keyword-wrangler.dev.sqlite
```

From now on, always start the server as follows, from the root folder of the project:

```
KW_ENV=dev node src/backend/index.js
```

14
Milestone 6 – Completing the Backend and Finalizing the Application

After starting the server in dev mode, have a look at `http://localhost:8080/`. You should now see the frontend with the sample data.

Playing around with this frontend quickly reveals that we are still lacking the API backend operations needed to create, update, and delete keyword entries. Let's fix that.

Creating the route for adding new keywords

Creating a new keyword results in a `POST` request to `/api/keywords`. Let's extend our spec accordingly:

 For the sake of brevity, I'm only showing the additional `it` block instead of the whole `spec` file.

```
it('should create a new keyword when receiving a POST request at \
  /api/keywords/', function (done) {
    var expected = {
      "_items": [
        {'id': 1, 'value':  'Aubergine', 'categoryID': 1},
        {'id': 2, 'value': 'Onion', 'categoryID': 1}
      ]
    };
```

```
var body = {
  'value': 'Onion',
  'categoryID': 1
};

async.series(
  [

    function(callback) {
      dbSession.insert(
        'category',
        {'name': 'Vegetable'},
        function(err) { callback(err) });
    },

    function(callback) {
      dbSession.insert(
        'keyword',
        {'value': 'Aubergine', 'categoryID': 1},
        function(err) { callback(err) });
    }

  ],

  function(err, results) {
    if (err) throw(err);
    request.post(
      {
        'url': 'http://localhost:8081/api/keywords/',
        'body': body,
        'json': true
      },
      function (err, res, body) {
        if (err) throw(err);
        expect(res.statusCode).toBe(200);
        request.get(
          {
            'url': 'http://localhost:8081/api/keywords/',
            'json': true
          },
          function (err, res, body) {
            expect(res.statusCode).toBe(200);
            expect(body).toEqual(expected);
            done();
          }

        );
      }
```

```
        );
      }

    );

  });
```

As you can see, this spec makes a complete round-trip. It adds the new keyword, and then makes a GET request to verify that the added keyword is contained in the list of all keywords.

Here is our trusty src/backend/server.js file updated with the code that is necessary to support the new POST operation:

```
'use strict';
var Percolator = require('percolator').Percolator;
var dbSession = require('../../src/backend/dbSession.js');

var Server = function(port) {
  var server = Percolator({'port': port, 'autoLink': false,\
 'staticDir': __dirname + '/../frontend'});

  server.route('/api/keywords',
    {
      GET: function (req, res) {
        dbSession.fetchAll('SELECT id, value, categoryID FROM keyword\
        ORDER BY id', function(err, rows) {
          if (err) {
            console.log(err);
            res.status.internalServerError(err);
          } else {
            res.collection(rows).send();
          }
        });
      },

      POST: function (req, res) {
        req.onJson(function(err, newKeyword) {
          if (err) {
            console.log(err);
            res.status.internalServerError(err);
          } else {
            dbSession.query('INSERT INTO keyword (value, categoryID) \
            VALUES (?, ?);', [newKeyword.value, newKeyword.categoryID],
            function (err)
            {
                if (err) {
                  console.log(err);
```

```
                              res.status.internalServerError(err);
                          } else {
                            res.object({'status': 'ok', 'id': \
                            dbSession.getLastInsertId()}).send();
                          }
                      });
                  }
              });
          }
        }
      );

      server.route('/api/keywords/categories',
      {
        GET: function (req, res) {
          dbSession.fetchAll('SELECT id, name FROM category ORDER BY \
          id', function(err, rows) {
            if (err) {
              console.log(err);
              res.status.internalServerError(err);
            } else {
              res.collection(rows).send();
            }
          });
        }
      }
    );

    return server;
};

module.exports = {'Server': Server};
```

As you can see in the `POST: function (req, res) {` line, we make use of Percolators `onJson` method, which provides us with the `POST` request body data in a very convenient way.

Creating the route for updating keywords

We also need to be able to save changes to an existing keyword entry. This is another `POST` request, this time at `/api/keywords/:i/*`. Here is the spec for this:

```
it('should update a keyword when receiving a POST request at \
/api/keywords/:id/', function (done) {
  var expected = {
```

```
"_items": [
{'id': 1, 'value': 'Onion', 'categoryID': 2} ] };
var body = {
  'id': 1,
  'value': 'Onion',
  'categoryID': 2
};

async.series(
  [

    function(callback) {
      dbSession.insert(
        'category',
        {'name': 'Vegetable'},
        function(err) { callback(err) });
    },

    function(callback) {
      dbSession.insert(
        'category',
        {'name': 'Utility'},
        function(err) { callback(err) });
    },

    function(callback) {
      dbSession.insert(
        'keyword',
        {'value': 'Aubergine', 'categoryID': 1},
        function(err) { callback(err) });
    }

  ],

    function(err, results) {
      if (err) throw(err);
      request.post(
      {
        'url': 'http://localhost:8081/api/keywords/1',
        'body': body,
        'json': true
      },
        function (err, res, body) {
          if (err) throw(err);
          expect(res.statusCode).toBe(200);
          request.get(
          {
            'url': 'http://localhost:8081/api/keywords/',
```

```
                      'json': true
                },
                function (err, res, body) {
                  expect(res.statusCode).toBe(200);
                  expect(body).toEqual(expected);
                  done();
                }
            );
          }
        );
      }

    );

  });
```

And here is the updated server code:

```
'use strict';
var Percolator = require('percolator').Percolator;
var dbSession = require('../../src/backend/dbSession.js');

var Server = function(port) {
  var server = Percolator({'port': port, 'autoLink': false, \
  staticDir':   __dirname + '/../frontend'});

  server.route('/api/keywords',
    {
      GET: function (req, res) {
        dbSession.fetchAll('SELECT id, value, categoryID FROM \
        keyword ORDER BY id',
        function(err, rows) {
          if (err) {
            console.log(err);
            res.status.internalServerError(err);
          } else {
            res.collection(rows).send();
          }
        });
      },

      POST: function (req, res) {
        req.onJson(function(err, newKeyword) {
          if (err) {
            console.log(err);
            res.status.internalServerError(err);
          } else {
```

```
                  dbSession.query('INSERT INTO keyword (value, categoryID) \
                  VALUES (?, ?);',    [newKeyword.value, \
                  newKeyword.categoryID], function (err) {
                    if (err) {
                      console.log(err);
                      res.status.internalServerError(err);
                    } else {
                      res.object({'status': 'ok', 'id': \
                      dbSession.getLastInsertId()}).send();
                    }
                  });
              }
            });
        }
      }
    );

server.route('/api/keywords/categories',
    {
      GET: function (req, res) {
        dbSession.fetchAll('SELECT id, name FROM category ORDER BY \
        id', function (err, rows) {
          if (err) {
            console.log(err);
            res.status.internalServerError(err);
          } else {
            res.collection(rows).send();
          }
        });
      }
    }
  );

server.route('/api/keywords/:id',
    {
      POST: function(req, res) {
        var keywordId = req.uri.child();
        req.onJson(function(err, keyword) {
          if (err) {
            console.log(err);
            res.status.internalServerError(err);
          } else {
            dbSession.query('UPDATE keyword SET value = ?, categoryID\
            = ? WHERE keyword.id = ?;', [keyword.value, \
            keyword.categoryID, keywordId], function (err, result) {
            if (err) {
            console.log(err);
            res.status.internalServerError(err);
```

```
            } else {
              res.object({'status': 'ok'}).send();
            }
          });
        }
      });
    }
  }
);

return server;
};

module.exports = {'Server': Server};
```

 Note how we handle the /api/keywords/categories route first, and then the /api/keywords/:id route. This is important, because if the /api/keywords/:id route would be defined first, it would handle /api/keywords/categories requests, interpreting categories as the :id.

Creating the route for deleting keywords

Now it's time for the final step. We need to add route handling for DELETE requests, and our application is complete.

Once again, we start with the spec:

```
it('should remove a keyword when receiving a DELETE request at \
/api/keywords/: id/', function (done){
  var expected = {
    "_items": [
      {'id': 1, 'value': 'Aubergine', 'categoryID': 1}
    ]
  };
  async.series(
    [

      function(callback) {
        dbSession.insert(
          'category',
          {'name': 'Vegetable'},
          function(err) { callback(err) });
      },
```

```
        function(callback) {
          dbSession.insert(
            'keyword',
            {'value': 'Aubergine', 'categoryID': 1},
            function(err) { callback(err) });
          },

          function(callback) {
            dbSession.insert(
            'keyword',
            {'value': 'Onion', 'categoryID': 1},
            function(err) { callback(err) });
          }

        ],

        function(err, results) {
          if (err) throw(err);
          request.del(
            {
              'url': 'http://localhost:8081/api/keywords/2/',
              'json': true
            },
            function (err, res, body) {
              if (err) throw(err);
              request.get(
              {
                'url': 'http://localhost:8081/api/keywords/',
                'json': true
              },
              function (err, res, body) {
                expect(res.statusCode).toBe(200);
                expect(body).toEqual(expected);
                done();
              }
            );
          }
        );
      }

    );

  });
```

Then, we extend the server code:

```
'use strict';
var Percolator = require('percolator').Percolator;
var dbSession = require('../../src/backend/dbSession.js');

var Server = function(port) {
  var server = Percolator({'port': port, 'autoLink': false, 'staticDir':\
__dirname + '/../frontend'});

  server.route('/api/keywords',
    {
      GET: function (req, res) {
        dbSession.fetchAll('SELECT id, value, categoryID FROM keyword\
        ORDER BY id',
        function(err, rows) {
          if (err) {
            console.log(err);
            res.status.internalServerError(err);
          } else {
            res.collection(rows).send();
          }
        });
      },

      POST: function (req, res) {
        req.onJson(function(err, newKeyword) {
          if (err) {
            console.log(err);
            res.status.internalServerError(err);
          } else {
            dbSession.query('INSERT INTO keyword (value, categoryID)\
            VALUES (?, ?);', [newKeyword.value,
            newKeyword.categoryID], function (err) {
              if (err) {
                console.log(err);
                res.status.internalServerError(err);
              } else {
                res.object({'status': 'ok', 'id': \
                bSession.getLastInsertId()}).send();
              }
            });
          }
        });
      }
    }
  );
```

```
server.route('/api/keywords/categories',
{
   GET: function (req, res) {
      dbSession.fetchAll('SELECT id, name FROM category ORDER BY \
      id', function(err, rows) {
         if (err) {
            console.log(err);
            res.status.internalServerError(err);
         } else {
            res.collection(rows).send();
         }
      });
   }
}
);

server.route('/api/keywords/:id',
  {
     POST: function(req, res) {
        var keywordId = req.uri.child();
        req.onJson(function(err, keyword) {
           if (err) {
              console.log(err);
              res.status.internalServerError(err);
           } else {
              dbSession.query('UPDATE keyword SET value = ?, categoryID\
              = ? WHERE keyword.id = ?;', [keyword.value, \
              keyword.categoryID, keywordId], function (err, result) {
                 if (err) {
                    console.log(err);
                    res.status.internalServerError(err);
                 } else {
                 res.object({'status': 'ok'}).send();
              }
           });
        }
     });
  },

DELETE: function(req, res) {
   var keywordId = req.uri.child();
   dbSession.query('DELETE FROM keyword WHERE keyword.id = ?;', \
   [keywordId], function(err, result) {
     if (err) {
        console.log(err);
        res.status.internalServerError(err);
     } else {
        res.object({'status': 'ok'}).send();
```

```
        }
      });
    }
  }
);

return server;
};

module.exports = {'Server': Server};
```

We can now restart the backend server (remember, KW_ENV=dev!), and with this, we should be able to fully enjoy all the operations our frontend provides.

Summary

In this chapter, we created a complete web-based CRUD application. It consists of a Node.js backend and an AngularJS frontend, connected through a RESTful web service API. We learned how to create a continuous delivery environment where end-to-end specs provide a tests suite that verifies the correctness of the web service API and a migrations setup ensures that database schema and code are in sync. The application can be run in the context of different configuration environments, allowing to keep test, dev, and production data separated.

Index

www.ingramcontent.com/pod-product-compliance
Lightning Source LLC
La Vergne TN
LVHW081343050326
832903LV00024B/1277